KEYS TO PARENTING YOUR ANXIOUS CHILD

Second Edition

Katharina Manassis, M.D., F.R.C.P.(C)
Hospital for Sick Children
Toronto

BARRON'S

All inquiries should be addressed to:
Barron's Educational Series, Inc.
250 Wireless Boulevard
Hauppauge, New York 11788
www.barronseduc.com

Library of Congress Catalog Card No.: 2007041028

ISBN-13: 978-0-7641-3916-1
ISBN-10: 0-7641-3916-9

Library of Congress Cataloging-in-Publication Data
Manassis, Katharina.
   Keys to parenting your anxious child / Katharina Manassis.
— 2nd ed.
      p.   cm. — (Barron's parenting keys)
   Includes index.
   ISBN-13: 978-0-7641-3916-1 (alk. paper)
   ISBN-10: 0-7641-3916-9 (alk. paper)
   1. Anxiety in children. 2. Adjustment (Psychology) in children. 3. Parenting. I. Title.

BF723.A5M36   2008
649'.154—dc22   2007041028

PRINTED IN THE UNITED STATES OF AMERICA
9 8 7 6 5 4 3 2

CONTENTS

Introduction   v

Part One—Why Are Children Anxious?
1   The Range of Childhood Anxieties   3
2   The Origins of Sensitivity   7
3   How Anxiety Develops   10
4   The Fearful Child   15

Part Two—How to Help Children Cope
5   Building Confidence   21
6   Techniques for Desensitization   28
7   Questions About Desensitization   32
8   Incentives for "Brave" Behavior   36
9   Questions About Incentive Systems   41
10 Defiant Behavior and Disincentives   45
11 The Child Who Worries   48
12 Helping Worried Children Cope   55
13 Getting Children to Cope Alone   60
14 Relieving Physical Stress   65
15 Relaxing the Mind   70
16 Diet, Exercise, and Sleep   73
17 Change and the Sensitive Child   78
18 When to Consider Medication   83
19 Specific Medications for Anxiety   88
20 Combining Techniques   94
21 Choosing Techniques   99

Part Three—Specific Problems

22	Anxiety at Different Ages	105
23	The Clingy Child	111
24	School Refusal and Panic	115
25	Shyness and Silence	120
26	Unassertiveness	126
27	Obsessions and Rituals	129
28	Other Unusual Habits	134
29	Perfectionism, Delaying, and Lying	137
30	When the Danger Is Real	142

Part Four—Others' Reactions to Anxiety

31	Family Interactions Around Anxiety	147
32	Being Consistent	153
33	Dealing with the Community	159
34	Dealing with Professionals	165
35	What If You're Still Struggling?	170

Appendix

Questions and Answers	174
Glossary	177
Resources for Helping Your Anxious Child	178
Index	182

INTRODUCTION

Childhood anxieties are not as transient or harmless as once believed. Anxious children are distressed by their inability to cope as well as other children do, which can have long-term effects on their confidence and self-esteem. Parents who try to help these children are often told they are "overreacting" or "overprotective," especially if their children are not misbehaving or otherwise drawing attention to themselves. Even some professionals may be unfamiliar with childhood anxieties, resulting in incorrect diagnoses and ineffective treatments.

Information for parents of anxious children is sparse. Books on behavior management can be helpful, but the strategies described may have to be modified for the anxious child. Books written about anxiety disorders in adults can also provide useful information, but the principles they describe are clearly designed for adults and may be difficult to apply to young children. As a child psychiatrist, I have found myself repeatedly referring parents to both of these sources of information, only to watch them struggle to discern what is relevant to their child. This book was written to ease that struggle. It will be useful for parents, teachers, and all those who work with anxious or sensitive children and their families.

Anxious children can be helped to overcome their difficulties, and parents are an important part of the solution. The principles of helping children cope with anxiety are simple and require no previous training. Furthermore, nobody is more of an expert on your child than you. Studies have shown that when anxious children are treated by professionals without parental involvement, children have difficulty applying the coping skills they learn to situations outside the therapist's office.

Also, if your child is affected only mildly by anxiety, getting help with the problem at home may feel more natural and less embarrassing for the child than being dragged off to a psychiatrist or psychologist. Keep in mind too that most therapists will spend 1 or 2 hours per week with your child. A teacher will spend perhaps 30 hours per week. That leaves 136 hours for you, the parents! What you do with that time can make a big difference to your child.

For some parents, this last sentence raises a disturbing question: "Are you implying that it's the parents' fault if the child is anxious?" The answer is a definite no. A number of factors can contribute to anxiety or alleviate it, and many of these factors have nothing to do with your child-rearing practices. Furthermore, trying to blame someone for the problem rarely helps to solve it. In the past, many treatments for anxious children have been unsuccessful precisely because professionals have tended to see parents as part of the problem rather than part of the solution.

This book is divided into short chapters called Keys. It can be used in several ways. Some of you will read it cover to cover, others will zero in immediately on the Key pertaining to their child, and still others will flip back and forth from one topic of interest to another. Below is a brief description of how the book is organized, so you can decide for yourself how to use it best.

Part One describes childhood anxieties and how they develop. Part Two describes the techniques parents can use to help their children cope with anxiety, including ways of selecting techniques and combining them. Part Three describes some specific anxiety-related problems commonly observed in children and ways to deal with each using the techniques described earlier. Although the book is intended mainly for parents of anxious children of about 7 to 12 years, a Key on parenting older and younger anxious children is included (Key 22). When there is a corresponding psychiatric disorder (usually, the most severe form of that particular problem), its name is provided in that Key as well. Finally, Part Four describes how to help your child in relation to the family, the school, professionals, and the larger community.

In each Key, information about the topic is discussed, one or more examples are provided, and key points are listed. Answers to some common questions asked by parents are also provided. All names and some details have been altered to protect confidentiality.

Treat the techniques described like a set of tools, rather than a recipe. You may not be able to match your child's behavior exactly to one particular Key. Even if you can, your child may not respond exactly like the child described in the Key does. Therefore, try to keep an open mind about a variety of techniques. If one doesn't work for your child, another may. Also, remember that your child is continually growing and developing. What works today may not work next month or next year, and vice versa. The more tools at your disposal, the better the chances of helping your child cope with a variety of challenges over time.

This book is written for parents of all children who have some sensitivity, whether mild, moderate, or extreme. If your child is only mildly affected (as shown by brief and only mildly disabling episodes of anxiety), the advice given in this book may be all you need to help your child. If your child is more seriously affected, this book should offer a useful adjunct to any professional treatment you may seek. At the very least, it will make you a more knowledgeable consumer of mental health services for your anxious child.

Acknowledgments

The belief that parents can find helpful solutions for their anxious children is based on another important fact: Parents helped in writing this book! In developing the Anxiety Disorders Clinic at our hospital, I have had the privilege of working with several hundred families of anxious children. Many of the parents from these families participated in a group program to learn how to better help their children cope with anxiety. These parents not only helped each other in the groups but also helped me by reading earlier versions of this book and making suggestions for its improvement. The team of clinicians I work with has also been invaluable in helping me learn more about helping anxious children and their families.

PART ONE

WHY ARE
CHILDREN ANXIOUS?

1

THE RANGE OF CHILDHOOD ANXIETIES

Jason was a bright six year old with an irresistible grin who enjoyed soccer and swimming, played well with his brother (for the most part), and was already beating his father at some computer games. His mother appreciated Jason's willingness to help around the house and commented on his gentle manner with pets. She had only one concern about her son: his unwillingness to try anything new. New jeans would "feel funny," unfamiliar music would "get on his nerves," and a new flavor of Jell-O was guaranteed to receive the verdict "Ick!" When introduced to potential playmates, Jason ignored them or only occasionally glanced in their direction. It took him a long time to "warm up." Knowing her son, Jason's mother made sure he met his first-grade teacher well before the school year started. Still, there were some tearful mornings in September before he adjusted.

———

Jenny had been unable to eat for a few days. She was seen in a pediatric clinic for a psychiatric consultation. Her pediatrician's request for the consultation said simply "Query eating disorder." He wondered if she had Anorexia Nervosa.

Jenny was a slim ten year old with long dark hair who withdrew shyly when the psychiatrist walked into the room. After some reassurance that she was not about to have her blood taken or be put through some other painful procedure, she gradually began to talk about her "eating problem." She admitted to feeling frightened whenever she put food into her mouth. She wasn't sure exactly why. She was ashamed that she couldn't do something as simple as eat and felt bad about the grief it caused her parents, but whenever she wanted to swallow she was stopped by her fear. She hated being thin and desperately wanted to be "just like everyone else."

Eventually, it became clear that her fear was of vomiting in public. It had started with not being able to eat in front of other children at school but had recently progressed to not being able to eat at all. Jenny did not have Anorexia Nervosa. She had a severe anxiety disorder.

What do Jason and Jenny have in common? At first glance, not very much. About the only similarity is that both had difficulty coping with some aspect of school, but Jason's difficulty was far less persistent and far less disabling than Jenny's. However, Jenny can be understood as having a more severe form of the same problem Jason experiences. Both children have difficulty coping because they are overly sensitive or anxious compared with most other children of their age.

The term *sensitive* is appropriate because it provides an accurate description of children like Jason and Jenny without making them sound psychiatrically disturbed (because most of them are not). Nevertheless, the terms *anxious* and *sensitive* will be used somewhat interchangeably in this book.

Severity of Childhood Anxieties

Jason and Jenny represent two ends of a range of severity for anxiety-related problems. At the mild end are children who resemble Jason in having some sensitive traits (about 10 percent of children). The most common of these traits is difficulty adjusting to changes and new situations. At the severe end are children who are more persistently impaired by their anxiety, as Jenny is (about 2 percent of children), and the rest are in between. Anxiety about going to school, fear of sleeping alone, difficulty making friends because of shyness, fear of speaking in public, and a tendency to worry a great deal about upcoming events (for example, school tests) are some common problems in the middle of the range.

In children at the extremely anxious end of the spectrum, there is often a family history of anxiety disorders in several generations, and the children themselves have been anxious for many months or even years. Some of the examples in this book refer to these children and so may sound a bit dramatic compared with your child's experiences. Many parents, however, have children who are *somewhat* anxious or sensitive at some point in their development. Fortunately, the principles for helping these children are the same as those used with their more extreme peers. The only differences are that mildly anxious children are less likely to require an extensive psychological or psychiatric assessment, less likely to require medication, and more likely to respond to parental interventions alone. Thus, the techniques described in this book may be all that is needed for a child like Jason. For one like Jenny, the techniques can be used to complement and increase the effectiveness of help provided by professionals.

If you feel, as a parent, that helping a child like Jenny would be an overwhelming task, try this simple exercise. First, think of a situation in which you felt anxious yourself but were able to manage. How did you cope? What did you say to yourself? What did you do? Now, imagine you are trying to help Jenny with her fear of vomiting. What could you say to her to reduce that fear? What could Jenny learn to say to herself when she is anxious? What could Jenny's parents do that might be helpful? What could Jenny learn to do herself that might be helpful?

Think of as many answers to these questions as you can. Have your spouse or partner do the same. Between the two of you, how many helpful suggestions have you found? Many parents are surprised by their ability to find helpful suggestions even for a severely anxious child like Jenny. If your children are more mildly anxious, your chances of being helpful to them are even greater!

2

THE ORIGINS OF
SENSITIVITY

Human beings in the past lived in a very unpredictable world. To hunt and gather food, they had to venture away from shelter. They often faced sudden danger. Those who could respond to danger quickly by fighting off an attacker or running away tended to survive. Slow responders were often not so lucky.

Human beings therefore developed an automatic response mechanism for dangerous situations. Characterized by physical, psychological, and emotional aspects, this response is often called the *fight-or-flight reaction*, because it developed originally to help human beings do just that. The sympathetic nervous system and its hormones, such as adrenaline, generate the physical response. The heart beats faster and more forcefully. Blood flow is directed to the large muscles, away from the hands, feet, and internal organs. The pupils enlarge. Breathing becomes faster. In every way, the body is prepared for action. Psychologically, there is a sense of great urgency. Thinking is rapid and focused on the danger present. Fear and anger are the emotions associated with this state.

When the danger passes, body and mind return to their resting state. Relaxation is produced by the parasympathetic nervous system (the opposite of the sympathetic nervous system).

The memory of the dangerous situation remains, however, providing the person with an "early warning system" for danger. In the future, that situation where danger was first encountered will again bring on the fight-or-flight reaction, even if the original danger is no longer present. Also, the mind's ability to imagine future events allows it to anticipate situations where the danger might recur. Usually, such situations resemble the original, dangerous one. Anticipation can bring on a fight-or-flight reaction, resulting in avoidance of these potentially dangerous situations. Eventually, the original dangerous incident may be forgotten, but the related situations still produce a fight-or-flight reaction. This accounts for the inability of many people to say what exactly is making them anxious in certain situations.

Most of the time, this early warning system is highly adaptive. In the past, humans with a sensitive system were better than their peers at avoiding danger and thus increased their chances of surviving long enough to reproduce. Accordingly, sensitivity became a trait that was passed on through the generations.

Unfortunately, sensitivity has its disadvantages too. People whose sympathetic nervous system is activated by situations where the risk of harm is nonexistent or only minimal lead very stressful lives. About 10 percent of the population struggle with this excessive sensitivity. In these people, the part of the brain responsible for emotions (the amygdala) has an unusually low threshold for fear. Brain imaging studies show unusually strong reactions in the amygdala when these people are shown angry, presumably threatening faces. Their excessive experience of fear is upsetting and results in the unnecessary avoidance of normal, day-to-day situations that other people consider not stressful or only mildly stressful.

It is this exaggerated fear when danger is nonexistent or minimal that is called *anxiety*.

For example, the fear of touching an element on a hot stove after you've been burned is useful and realistic. However, anxiety about touching the entire stove is unrealistic and disabling, leaving you perpetually dependent on restaurants and take-out food. Years later, you may have forgotten the minor burn you received but still feel vaguely uncomfortable near the stove.

Sensitivity and Your Child

You may wonder how these ideas apply to your child. We all vary in our sensitivity to becoming anxious, and some anxious people suffer more than others. The 10 percent of the population considered unusually sensitive probably don't have a discrete illness but merely a greater than average predisposition to becoming anxious. In stressful situations, unusually sensitive people can experience a variety of anxiety-related problems. The most common ones occurring in children are described in this book.

Don't worry if your child has several of the problems discussed. This does not necessarily indicate severe anxiety. The description of each problem is based on a cluster of symptoms that psychiatrists have observed, and a great deal of overlap exists between the clusters. Having several problems may be no worse than having one.

The key question to determine severity is, How much does the anxiety interfere with the child's ability to engage in age-appropriate activities? When a problem persists and stops a child from participating in activities that other children of the same age enjoy, help is required. Using the techniques described in this book, parents can provide much of that help.

3

HOW ANXIETY DEVELOPS

About 10 percent of the population is unusually sensitive to any sign of danger. This trait can be identified in children as young as 21 months, suggesting that it is likely to be an aspect of the child's inborn temperament. At 21 months, these children react to any new situation as if it were dangerous. They show extreme caution, avoiding almost all new people or new situations. This trait, first described by Jerome Kagan, Ph.D., at Harvard University, has been termed *behavioral inhibition,* because the usual tendency for young children to explore their surroundings appears inhibited in children with this trait. When a group of such children were observed over several years, it was found that a higher than average proportion of them developed clinical anxiety disorders later.

Recall, though, that only 2 or 3 percent of apparently inhibited children develop significant anxiety disorders. What happens to the other 7 or 8 percent? They learn to cope. They learn to do all the things other children their age do despite their inhibited temperament. They may have a harder time than their peers, especially in situations involving a lot of unpredictability and change, but they adjust.

The Role of Early Relationships

An inhibited child may not develop an anxiety disorder if that child feels supported and develops good coping skills. Support and coping seem to go hand in hand, as preschoolers who have a predictably supportive relationship with their mothers (as shown by experiments in which these preschoolers are distressed when briefly separated from their mothers and quickly reassured when their mothers return) show better coping skills and less anxiety than those who do not have a predictably supportive relationship. This appears to hold true even if the mother is herself anxious.

The basis of such relationships is parents' ability to read their children's distress signals sensitively and respond to them consistently. Children growing up with such parents become confident that these people can soothe their distress and will be there for them predictably. Using the parental example, children are able eventually to develop their own coping skills. The more successfully children cope, the more confidence develops. Life no longer looks like a minefield for them. Instead, it becomes an adventure to be explored.

Even if your early relationship with your sensitive child was not predictably supportive, you haven't missed the boat. First of all, developing such a relationship can be hard for even the best parent if the child's temperament is particularly difficult. Second, infants with less than ideal early relationships can develop good coping skills later. The human brain shows a remarkable ability to compensate for early deficits. Therefore, your child can still be helped to learn coping skills, and the earlier you start, the better.

Before you start, check with the family doctor or pediatrician to determine if there could be a medical reason for the anxiety. Thyroid problems and certain medications can sometimes mimic anxiety problems. Learning problems can also mimic anxiety and should be suspected in children who are mainly anxious about school work. In addition, children with nonverbal learning disabilities can show extreme sensitivity to change or perceived unfairness (with tantrums in response) that may be mistaken for anxiety. Children with developmental delays or socially odd behavior in addition to anxiety are sometimes suffering from a mild form of autism. Each of these conditions requires different treatment, so it is worth taking the time to get a clear diagnosis.

If anxiety is present together with another mental health problem, for example a problem with attention or misbehavior, the doctor can help decide which problem needs to be dealt with first. Typically, children's anxieties do not readily improve as long as their behavior is out of control. When children are able to lash out at others when distressed, they are usually not motivated to learn to cope in other ways. Similarly, problems with attention (found in up to a quarter of anxious children) can make it difficult for children to learn coping strategies for managing their anxiety. After these problems are addressed, some children appear less anxious, perhaps because they have fewer negative interactions with parents, teachers, and other adults. If anxiety persists, however, it can be effectively treated at that point.

The Balance Between Sensitivity and Coping

Sensitive children who feel secure in their families can still become anxious. For the sensitive child, the development of anxiety depends on the balance between (a) innate vulnerability to anxiety and (b) support and coping skills. Highly vulnerable children may develop anxiety disorders even with excellent family supports. Children with less innate vulnerability may develop anxiety disorders only if they are abused or suffer other serious traumas. These children often require therapy to address their traumas in addition to learning the coping skills described in this book. It is more common to see children who maintain a balance between vulnerability and coping and support until some stressful event triggers an anxiety disorder. Anxiety disorders are equally common among boys and girls before puberty, but they are more common in girls in adolescence.

In the figure below, the process of developing an anxiety disorder is compared to an unbalanced teeter-totter. To restore the balance, one could reduce the stress, increase the support, or increase the coping skills; innate vulnerability is unlikely to change.

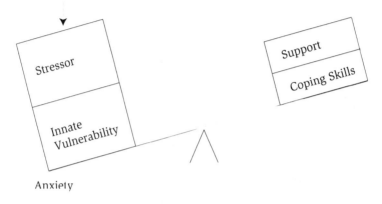

Figure 1

Reducing stress can include creating more regular, predictable routines. For example, in divorced families, children do better if they see each parent on a consistent schedule and transitions from one home to the other don't occur every day. Unpredictable behavior by adults is also frightening for children, so limiting displays of conflict or hostility in front of children is another important way to reduce their stress. Anxious children can also be stressed by having too much stimulation in the environment. For example, anxious children with multiple after-school programs and lessons can sometimes benefit from a reduced number of such activities. Television programs and video games can also be overly stimulating, especially during the last hour or so before bedtime, so should be limited in the evenings.

In the long run, however, a parent cannot always be there to support the child and protect that child from all stress. If continuously sheltered in this way, the child would later be unable to function in the adult world. This is why *coping* is so important.

Anxiety over the Life Span

Parents often wonder if anxious children outgrow their anxiety or if they get worse over time. Some children, if encouraged to face their fears, develop coping skills on their own as they mature. In that sense, they do "outgrow" their fears. On the other hand, children who avoid their fears can become quite disabled by them. With prolonged avoidance of age-appropriate activities, valuable skills are lost and these children can become increasingly dependent on family members. Often, family conflicts result. With increased family conflict and decreased ability to keep up at school and with peers, their self-esteem often decreases.

Fortunately, most anxious children can overcome their fears by gradually facing them. Each time a feared situation is faced, the child becomes a little less sensitive to it. After a child is repeatedly exposed to the feared situation and is helped to successfully master his anxiety, his fight-or-flight reaction to that situation will disappear.

Over a lifetime, anxiety tends to come and go in those people who are predisposed to it (the "innate vulnerability" of Figure 1). *Coping skills do not "cure" anxiety.* Exacerbations tend to happen when supports are lost or a new stressor is faced. For example, the expectation for children to behave more independently at adolescence can be difficult for a sensitive child who has previously relied a great deal on parental support. For a child who has learned coping skills, however, this difficulty is not a cause for despair. Instead, it is a signal that previously learned coping skills need to be reviewed, and a few new ones may need to be added. Each time a new situation is mastered, confidence builds, allowing the child to face new challenges and live a productive, fulfilling life.

4

THE FEARFUL CHILD

Fears are the most common problem related to sensitivity in children. Many children experience the fear of a particular thing or a particular situation at some point in their development. Some fears can even be considered normal aspects of development. For example, babies usually develop a fear of strangers when they are about nine months old. This fear is considered normal and a healthy sign of the baby's developing ability to distinguish familiar people (like the mother or the father) from unfamiliar people.

Similarly, some fears occur in many children at certain ages. For example, two- or three-year-olds are often afraid of being alone in the dark. They may appear confident and even adventurous as long as they can see a parent, but in the dark this source of reassurance disappears and they behave like much younger children. Eight- or nine-year-olds may worry about death. It is around this age that children become more aware of concepts related to time. Thus, unlike younger children, they are able to understand death as a permanent thing and become frightened of it. Some psychology texts provide lists of common fears for each age. Whether or not a particular fear is "normal," however, depends less on what the books say than on what effect it has on your child.

Fears become problematic when they occur outside the context of normal development and interfere with the child's ability to cope with life the way other children of the same age do. The following is an example of one such fear.

Six-year-old Mary went with her father to the pet store in the mall. She saw a large, furry dog and her cute, furry puppies. Mary leaned down, and before anyone could stop her she reached into the dog cage to pet the adorable puppies. The protective mother dog immediately bit Mary's hand. Mary shrieked in pain and was whisked away to the nearest hospital. She experienced a strong fight-or-flight reaction, accompanied by fear and anger (after all, she wasn't trying to hurt the puppies—how unfair!).

The wound was minor, and the fight-or-flight reaction soon subsided. However, the memory of the large, biting dog at the pet store in the mall remained. At the sight of pet stores or large dogs, Mary cried and again experienced a fight-or-flight reaction. The fear spread to include all dogs, regardless of their size. Anticipating danger, Mary avoided the mall altogether. Eventually, the incident at the pet store was forgotten but a persistent dread of shopping malls and dogs remained. Mary would not go near either one of them.

Most parents reading this story will think, "That doesn't sound so unusual. Wouldn't any child react that way?" It's true that reacting strongly to a dog bite and being temporarily fearful of dogs afterward is an expected reaction in most children. What distinguishes Mary, however, is the *persistence* of the fear and its *effect on normal activities*.

When Fears Become Phobias

The length of time a child is fearful can be a cause for concern. With the exception of extraordinary circumstances (for example, a child is abducted or lives through a war or natural disaster), most children recover from frightening events in a few days to a few weeks. Fears that continue to haunt a child for months or even years are more unusual. They begin to interfere with the child's ability to face normal developmental challenges. The toddler may stop playing with other children, feeling unsafe when farther than arm's length from a parent.

The school-age child who has just learned to ride a bicycle may stop "in case I run into a dog."

Eventually, the child's fear restricts day-to-day activities. In order to avoid dogs Mary may refuse to visit anyone who owns a dog, even if the animal is kept far away from her. Walking a block to the store may be avoided because of the small possibility of meeting a vicious dog. Worries about encountering dogs may become exhausting or affect Mary's concentration at school. Anxiety begins to affect life at home, at school, and with peers. The greater the discrepancy between a fearful child's behavior and that of other children of the same age, the more disabling the fear becomes.

Finally, the fear becomes unrealistic. In the example, Mary has lost some perspective on which situations are truly dangerous and which ones are not. When avoiding a shopping mall because of the off chance that there might be an unrestrained, vicious dog roaming about there, she is showing excessive caution. She is also underestimating her own ability to avoid further attack by taking some precautions that do make sense (for example, not reaching into cages). This tendency to overestimate danger and underestimate one's own strengths constitutes a distorted way of thinking common to anxious people of all ages. It also allows us to make a useful distinction:

Fear is a strong physical, mental, and emotional reaction to truly dangerous events.

Anxiety is a fearful reaction to events that are not dangerous or are significantly less dangerous than the fearful person imagines.

Thus, Mary's initial fearful, fight-or-flight reaction to being bitten is quite realistic under the circumstances. However, the prolonged avoidance of situations only slightly similar to the original one is not realistic. This unrealistic avoidance constitutes anxiety. If it becomes extreme and interferes with daily activity, it is called a *phobia*.

Events That Trigger Phobias

Children can be fearful without experiencing an extremely frightening event. Many parents cannot recall specific frightening events that account for their child's excessive caution or fearfulness. Some parents even worry that the child's behavior may be evidence of trauma or abuse that has occurred without their knowledge. If a child who has been happy, outgoing, and fearless for many years suddenly becomes fearful, there may be some justification for this worry. More commonly, however, the child has a history of cautiousness or sensitivity that goes back to the earliest years of life, suggesting an inborn vulnerability to fearfulness.

The temperamentally sensitive or inhibited children described earlier can become fearful in response to what for the average child is only a minor change in circumstances. For these children, even meeting a person who is dressed differently from people with whom the child is familiar may result in a fearful response. A group of such children were once introduced to a friendly research assistant dressed as a clown, and for weeks afterward parents demanded help to address the "clown phobia" inadvertently caused in their children. Almost any unusual sight, noise, smell, taste, or other sensation seems to result in a kind of sensory overload for these children, causing them to become upset and fearful. A whole group of such novel sensory experiences at once (for example, all the events involved in moving to a new house) is perceived as stressful or even traumatic. It is often after such events that these children show increased fearfulness that persists and interferes with daily activity. At this point, parents usually feel the need to do something.

PART TWO

HOW TO HELP
CHILDREN COPE

5

BUILDING CONFIDENCE

Paradoxically, fearful children may need to *behave* more confidently before they *feel* more confident. Children know when fear is preventing them from keeping up with their peers. In some cases, they may also experience teasing because of this. It is hard for such a child to believe parents who say, "You're just as good [or strong or capable] as anybody else," when there is no solid evidence for this statement and other children are calling the child names.

Giving children confidence consists of encouraging them to behave more confidently. Research with anxious people confirms that the only way to become less fearful is to face what is feared. Remember the old adage about falling off a horse? It's true. The best way to handle a frightening fall off a horse is to get right back in the saddle. The longer you wait, the harder it becomes to ride again. This is true for fearful children as well. Reassurance, figuring out what caused the fear, coping strategies, and other mental gymnastics can go just so far. Only facing fear can reduce it.

Desensitization

Facing what is feared results in a process called *desensitization*. The first time your child faces a feared situation, the result will be a dramatic fight-or-flight response, accompanied by a feeling of intense anxiety. If a frightened child remains in the feared situation until the fight-or-flight response subsides, however, the response will be less intense the next time that situation is faced. The third exposure will produce even less anxiety, and so on. Eventually, your child will be able to describe the feared situation as "no big deal" and may even deny ever fearing it in the first place.

An Encouraging Attitude

Key 6 describes a system for helping children face specific feared situations. For this system to work, however, it is important to adopt an *attitude that fearful children experience as encouraging.* Keeping this attitude in mind while talking to a fearful child will increase the chances that the child will try to face what is feared.

The following are three examples of statements intended to be encouraging. Admittedly, they are extreme versions of different styles of encouragement.

"There's nothing to be scared of, you silly child! Shape up!"

"The teacher wants you to go to school, so go ahead. But watch out for the traffic at the intersection, and don't talk to any strangers, and for heaven's sake call me at work if you're not sure you can handle it, and are you sure you feel OK about this?, and . . ."

"It must seem very scary, but I believe you can do it."

If you were anxious about something yourself, which approach would you find most encouraging?

In the first statement, the child's feelings are not acknowledged. The fear is dismissed as invalid, and the child is put down. This statement will make the child feel ashamed of being anxious, rather than feel encouraged.

In the second statement, the child's anxiety is acknowledged but magnified out of all proportion. The parent seems to identify with the child's anxiety and is making the teacher the heavy. This statement is unlikely to inspire confidence. If you don't believe your child can handle the feared situation, the child won't believe it either.

In the third statement, the child's feelings are acknowledged but the parent also expresses confidence in the child's abilities. The result is a child who feels understood but also ready to face a challenge. This constitutes true encouragement. Parents often ask whether to support or push their fearful child. Clearly, the answer is both. These children do best when parents show empathy for their feelings *and* express a belief in their ability to do what is feared.

What if the situation is too hard and your child panics?

Ideally, children should be encouraged to face situations that are challenging but not overwhelming for them. Most parents, however, occasionally misjudge what their child can manage. This need not be disastrous. Panic symptoms usually subside once the child leaves the situation and are never fatal. Praise your child for getting through the situation and reassure her that you'll try an easier situation, next time.

How do you tell if your child is getting better?

The simple answer is, When the child is more confident. But how do you quantify confidence? Many parents give up on trying to help their fearful child because they still hear statements like "I can't do it" even after months of working with the child.

Behavior tends to change before feelings do. It is also easier to measure. Therefore, keep a record of your child's fearful behaviors for at least a week before trying any of the techniques in this book. If you notice several fearful behaviors, select one or two that will be easy to monitor (preferably, ones that occur in front of you), because no parent can observe a child all day long. This record is called a *baseline*.

Be specific in your baseline description and record it. Include how often each behavior happens, how intensely your child reacts (on a scale from one to ten), how long it lasts, and how much support or reassurance from you is needed. Without these specifics, small changes that occur gradually may be missed. Watching for progress without an objective record can be a little like watching grass grow: You see nothing happening at the time, but if you wait a couple of weeks it is definitely taller. If you don't wait, you may think the techniques don't work. This results in giving up on helping the child and missing the opportunity to praise the child for progress that does occur.

Each time you try a new technique described in this book, again record your child's level of difficulty with the same behavior(s). By comparing the new level(s) with the baseline, you can tell whether or not progress is really taking place. Seeing change stops you from getting discouraged and provides the enjoyable opportunity to praise your child's progress. Praise builds confidence, which in turn encourages further progress. On the other hand, if there is no change this will be obvious as well. In this case, use the lack of change as a signal to stop what you are doing so that no further time is wasted on a technique that clearly isn't working.

Recall Key 4's description of Mary, the little girl who developed a fear of dogs. Before her parents intervened, Mary was already able to look at pictures of dogs, even though she would not go near a real dog without considerable crying. The specific description of her baseline behaviors read:

> "Mary can look at pictures of dogs smaller than a German shepherd (the dog that bit her) for five minutes without crying or turning away. She cries at pictures of bigger dogs (intensity: five out of ten) but settles down in two minutes when given lots of reassurance, including a hug. She panics (intensity: eight out of ten) at the sight of big dogs on

the street and won't settle down for an hour, but she can walk past smaller dogs calmly if there is a distance of about ten feet between herself and the dog."

In this case, signs of progress could include

- Looking at pictures of smaller dogs for more than five minutes
- Looking at pictures of bigger dogs for any length of time without crying or turning away
- Looking at pictures of bigger dogs but crying less intensely
- Looking at pictures of bigger dogs but settling down more quickly (less than two minutes)
- Looking at pictures of bigger dogs, crying, but settling down with less reassurance
- A less extreme reaction to seeing a big dog (decreased fear intensity)
- Settling down more quickly (less than an hour) after seeing a big dog
- Leaving fewer than ten feet between herself and a smaller dog

Thus, Mary can demonstrate progress in at least eight ways, and there are lots of opportunities for praise and encouragement. Usually, parents will not watch for this many signs of change but instead set a specific goal and chart the child's progress toward that goal. Mary's goal was to eventually pet a dog who lived next door. She was encouraged to approach this goal in small steps, regardless of how upset she got. Making the goal a *positive* behavior is usually best, because focusing too much on negative behavior tends to encourage it. Keys 6 to 9 describe this approach in more detail. If you spot a sign of progress that isn't part of the child's goal, praise it anyway! Praise never hurts.

Before you start, decide which one or two behaviors are most important. More than this would be too confusing for your child and too time-consuming for you. Start with behaviors that you can readily observe and that you (and preferably your child also) will be motivated to work on for a while. Don't pick the behavior that is likely to be most difficult for your child to change, though. Practice on easier ones first, until you feel comfortable with the techniques. The figure below shows a behavior chart for Mary that encourages approaching the dog next door by looking at a picture of him and looking at him from behind the fence.

GETTING TO KNOW REX (The Dog Next Door)							
	SUN	MON	TUES	WED	THURS	FRI	SAT
Looking at picture × 5 min.	✓	✓		✓	✓		✓
Looking from behind fence				✓		✓	

Update your record frequently. Ideally, record the chosen behavior (and all of its characteristics) every time it occurs. If this is unrealistic, try to record it within a day, while the details are still fresh in your mind.

If you have a spouse or partner, work together to ensure consistency. For starters, check that both of you are recording the same behaviors in the same way. Once you have recorded the initial baseline, take some time to talk with your partner about how you plan to help your child. Regardless of the techniques you choose, the best plan is one you can both agree on and follow. Set a weekly time for the two of you to look back on the record in order to evaluate progress and fine-tune your approach.

Changes in behavior often follow a "two steps forward, one step back" progression. Don't be discouraged if your child has a rough few days or even a rough week, as long as the overall trend is toward improvement.

When progress does occur, share the information with your child. Just like their parents, fearful children can have difficulty recognizing when they are improving. Knowing progress is being made and having it recognized by you will help your child to be hopeful and to keep trying. Try to ignore setbacks—fearful children are usually hard enough on themselves when setbacks occur and don't need to be reminded about them by their parents.

6

TECHNIQUES FOR DESENSITIZATION

Desensitization to feared situations can occur in two ways: (a) sudden exposure, also called *flooding,* and (b) gradual exposure, also called *systematic desensitization.* Sudden exposure works faster but is more stressful.

Flooding

Let's return one more time to the example of Mary. Suppose Mary's parents wanted to help her overcome the fear of dogs. The fastest way to overcome the fear would be to have her go to a kennel and stay there until the fear subsided. The experience would be very stressful for Mary but, if tolerated, would desensitize her immediately.

Systematic Desensitization

Using a more gradual approach, Mary's parents could start by having her look at a picture of a dog, then look at a real dog from a distance, then get progressively closer to the dog, then pet the dog, and finally engage in an activity in a room with dogs while ignoring them (continuously looking at what is feared is often the last anxious behavior to go). Thus, a series of small steps can be designed, starting with the easiest and working up to the most difficult. Encouragement, praise, and an incentive system (discussed in Keys 8 and 9) may be added to increase the child's willingness to participate in this process.

When to Use Each Technique

Flooding is most effective in the case of small children with relatively mild fears. For example, a four-year-old boy was frightened at the supermarket when he saw a neighbor who had lost an arm to cancer. His parents invited the neighbor over for coffee, keeping the child in the same room. Before long, the child's fear turned into curiosity and the neighbor was soon considered a friend.

Unfortunately, older children have enough strength and speed to escape almost any flooding situation a parent can design. Occasionally, a highly motivated older child will voluntarily go into a flooding situation and use coping skills to remain there until the anxiety subsides. Few parents are lucky enough to have such a child. Therefore, in older children with persistent fears, a gradual desensitization system usually works better.

A Gradual Desensitization System

Start by thinking of a series of intermediate steps between your child's baseline and his or her full participation in the feared situation. The steps must be small enough for the child to have a reasonable chance of succeeding but large enough to keep the task challenging. Most people do best on any task when their anxiety level is mild to moderate but not extreme. With some thought, most parents can come up with at least four or five intermediate steps for each particular situation their child fears. It is common to make the first step too big, resulting in a high level of anxiety in the child. Therefore, if you're not sure where to start, begin with something the child is already doing occasionally and work on having the child do it more consistently.

Points to keep in mind include the following:

1. Give the child some say on when to move to the next step. This increases the child's sense of control, which further reduces fear and increases the chances of success. Your praise and encouragement, the child's pride

in a job well done, and incentives will increase the motivation to move on. Patiently encouraging even partial success usually works better than arguing to try to make the child do more.

2. The sooner the child faces the feared situation, the less opportunity exists for anticipatory anxiety to develop and the faster desensitization works. Don't be discouraged, though, if your child's anxiety has persisted for some time without treatment. You haven't missed the boat. Even long-standing fears can diminish within a few months if the child follows a planned, consistent desensitization program.

3. Desensitization works best if the exposures to the feared situation are not too far apart (daily is best). This may require some planning on your part, especially if the feared situation is not one your child normally faces every day. For example, the parents of the child with the dog phobia described earlier may need to speak to a friend who owns a dog about having their child visit the dog on a regular basis.

4. Allowing early escape from a feared situation while your child's anxiety is still high doesn't work. The relief from anxiety experienced with escape is intense. Consequently, the anxious child seeks that relief again and again by escaping subsequent anxiety-provoking situations. Desensitization then becomes nearly impossible, and the attempt to encourage it has backfired. On average, it takes about 20 minutes for anxiety to subside in a feared situation, so encourage your child to spend at least that amount of time every time a feared situation is faced.

5. Ensure that you are exposing the child to the *same* feared situation each time. This may sound obvious, but a number of parents have run into difficulty

because they varied the feared situation slightly with different exposures. For example, in working on a dog phobia exposure to a poodle is not the same as exposure to a German shepherd; exposure to an old, sedentary dog is not the same as exposure to a young, frisky one; and a planned exposure is not the same as unexpectedly seeing a dog on the street. In each case, the latter situation is usually more frightening.

In summary, an ideal desensitization treatment for most anxious children consists of daily exposures in small, manageable steps, beginning soon after the fear develops and lasting at least 20 to 30 minutes per exposure. Exposure once a week is a bare minimum for desensitization to occur.

7

QUESTIONS ABOUT DESENSITIZATION

What if my child fears something that doesn't happen every day (for example, getting a needle injection, going on an airplane, or going to a sleepover party)?

It's true that desensitization to rare events is more difficult, but it is still possible. Start by providing your child with detailed information about the event. Children with phobias usually try to plug their ears at this point. Be positive, however, about this first step toward desensitization. Encourage your child to listen, even if an incentive is required. If the child asks questions, answer them but do not expect the child to answer yours. The idea is to provide a regular, measured dose of realistic information, not to get into a debate. If the child becomes very distressed, stop and provide comfort or do one of the relaxation techniques with the child that are described later.

Once your child is comfortable with the information (usually after several daily talks), have your child do some relaxed breathing while imagining going into the feared situation. Encourage detailed visualization of every aspect of the situation. Once the situation has been mastered mentally, begin to take real steps toward it (for example, going near the doctor's office for the needle phobia, going to the airport for the airplane phobia, or spending some time during the day at the house where the sleepover is planned) and, using these real steps, carry on with desensitizing the child.

Some of the intermediate steps for desensitization may require creativity on your part. Examples include a child impaired by a fear of seeing others vomit on the bus or of encountering a flying insect. In each case, the feared situation is difficult to approximate. Some parents find visual representations of such events on the Internet, although some images are overly graphic and disturbing to children. Used carefully though, this can be one way of exposing the child to an approximation of the event. Another approach is to ask adult friends for suggestions. One mother of a girl with a flying insect phobia, for example, was surprised to find that her best friend's brother was a beekeeper and very willing to help her daughter safely confront this fear.

How much support should I provide for my child? For example, should I accompany my child into feared situations?

Many parents wonder about whether or not it is appropriate to accompany their child into feared situations. After all, the idea is to help the child become more independent rather than dependent, isn't it? The answer is, It depends on the plan you have made with the child. For example, you may decide that Step 1 will consist of exposure to a situation while you hold the child's hand, Step 2 will consist of exposure with you at a distance of a few feet, Step 3 will consist of exposure with you one block away, and the final step will consist of exposure in your absence. This is fine and should not increase your child's dependency on you. On the other hand, if you accompany your child because you are begged to do so and this is *not* part of the plan, the child learns that fears need not be faced alone as long as parents can be coerced into coming along. Clearly, this message increases dependency.

What if my child stops facing a situation he used to be able to handle?

All anxious children face occasional setbacks, so learn to expect them. Often, the child is going through a stressful time (for example, examinations at school), resulting in a generally heightened level of anxiety, and starts to avoid more situations. Other times, the situation is no longer interesting to the child. For example, a child may lose interest in performing at piano recitals, even when she is no longer anxious about them. Setbacks need only be concerning if they are accompanied by general withdrawal from enjoyable activities, or changes in mood, appetite, or sleep as these may be signs of depression. In this case, consult a mental health professional.

Assuming the setback is due to temporary stress, however, resist the temptation to criticize the child for failing to do something that was previously mastered or to ask, "Why can't you do it?" This is discouraging, and may prompt further setbacks. Instead, wait for the stress to pass. Sometimes, ignoring setbacks is the best way to overcome them! If the avoidance continues, empathically encourage the child to face the situation again. If this is difficult, go back to the desensitization steps that worked in the past. Keep a patient and optimistic attitude, and your child may eventually adopt it as well.

What about getting the child to talk about the anxious feelings. Won't that help?

Not necessarily. The notion that "getting your feelings out" solves all psychological problems is, unfortunately, a myth. Getting the child to talk about the anxious feelings may not work, for two reasons. First, anxious children are often unwilling or unable to talk about their fears. They may be unsure what is causing the fear and/or may be ashamed of the problem. Trying to force the child to talk about the feelings then becomes an exercise in frustration. Second, talking about anxious feelings sometimes makes them worse. This is particularly true in the case of the anxious child who tries to postpone facing scary situations by asking a series of "What if?" questions (see Key 11). The more parents try to reassure this child, the more "what if?" questions enter the child's mind. Eventually, the parents are left feeling inadequate and anxious themselves and the child avoids facing what is feared. A helpful way of talking to anxious children is described in Keys 11 to 13.

What if facing what is feared is so upsetting that the anxious child gets depressed or even attempts suicide?

This question is common among parents who are themselves somewhat anxious and lack confidence in their child's abilities. Anxious children do not become depressed or attempt suicide while facing their fears unless they have other serious psychological problems besides anxiety. In the long run, the sense of accomplishment that comes from facing fears boosts self-esteem and thus *reduces* the risk of depression.

If your child is getting discouraged by repeated unsuccessful attempts to face a particular situation, slow down. Start with what the child can do, and think of some intermediate steps to work up to the feared situation gradually. Even a small step may have to be broken down further into even smaller steps. It is important not to give up completely, since this can create a sense of helplessness in the child and thus reduce the chances of future success.

Note that adolescents who have panic attacks sometimes describe a sense of impending doom during an attack. They may *feel* as though they are about to die at such times and will say so. In this case, parents can offer the reassurance that panic attacks are not fatal and always come to an end. Panic attacks are described further in Key 24.

8

INCENTIVES FOR "BRAVE" BEHAVIOR

Most children will not voluntarily expose themselves to something they fear. In fact, many will fight strenuously to avoid facing situations they fear. Providing incentives for "brave" behaviors while placing less emphasis on anxious ones can increase a child's willingness to face anxiety-provoking situations.

Some fears are overcome through natural incentives. For example, a child may think, "The other kids will say I'm a baby if I can't do this," or "I hate going the doctor [or counselor]. If I can do this, I won't have to go there anymore." Some children overcome their fears using these incentives alone!

Parental praise is also an excellent incentive. Some anxious children are so eager to please their parents that they change their behavior in response to parental praise alone. Praise is most effective when the child is told specifically what was done well, rather than general statements such as "That was good." Try to find out what the child did or thought that allowed her to accomplish the task, and praise that strategy. This will increase the likelihood that the same strategy will be used again in the future, resulting in further success.

Incentive Systems

In addition to praise and natural incentives, anxious children may require a planned incentive system to overcome their fears. The reason for such a system is simple: People are more apt to do something if it has a pleasant consequence than if it has an unpleasant consequence. This principle can be applied in four possible ways:

To *increase* a *desirable* behavior, either

1. Provide something pleasant after it is done or
2. Remove something unpleasant after it is done.

Allowing a child to go out and play after completing homework is an example of providing something pleasant (play) after a desirable behavior (doing homework). If the child dislikes being alone in his room, allowing him to interact with others after completing the homework could also be seen as removing something unpleasant (being alone) after a desirable behavior (doing homework).

To *decrease* an *undesirable* behavior, either

1. Remove something pleasant when the child engages in the behavior, or
2. Provide something unpleasant when the child engages in the behavior.

Ignoring a child who is yelling can be seen as removing something pleasant (parental attention) when the child engages in undesirable behavior (yelling). Many parents apply this principle when giving their children five- or ten-minute time-outs in their rooms for misbehaving. Punishing a child who has misbehaved is an example of an unpleasant consequence.

Incentive systems often incorporate some material rewards. A common approach is awarding a gold star or sticker each time the desired behavior occurs. The stickers are collected to obtain a reward that child and parent have previously agreed upon. If the desired behavior does not occur, the sticker is not awarded and no further comment is made (to avoid reinforcing *not* earning stickers). A chart or calendar is used to keep track of the child's progress. To preserve family harmony, a parallel system may have to be designed for siblings, using another behavior but similar rewards. Just about every child has at least one behavior that can improve. Older children and adolescents may not respond to stickers, but most will value some form of reward (for example, extra computer time or a special privilege). If the incentive system is combined with gradual exposure, some parents choose to award more stickers for more difficult steps.

In overcoming her fear of dogs, Mary can be rewarded for each step in her gradual desensitization program: The first step (for example, looking at a picture of a dog) earns one point, the second step (for example, looking at a real dog from a distance) earns two points, the third step (for example, standing just a few feet away from a dog) earns three points, and so on. A modest reward (for example, a small coloring book) could be provided for every five points, and a larger one at the end of the desensitization program.

Incentive systems work best if

1. The behavior to be rewarded is clearly and specifically spelled out.

     For example, "being good" or "being brave" is not specific; "not crying or fussing for more than five minutes before leaving for school" is specific.
2. The reward offered is valued by the child.

     You know your child better than any expert. If your child responds better to earning playtime than to earning stickers, use playtime as a reward.
3. The reward occurs immediately (or as soon as possible) after the desired behavior is performed.

Children have a different sense of time from that of adults. A delay of even a few hours can seem like an eternity to a six year old and reduces the effectiveness of the incentive.

4. The system is simple and consistent.

Most effective systems focus on one or two behaviors at a time. Anything more than that gets too complicated for the child and too time-consuming for the parent who is monitoring the behaviors.

To be consistent, respond in exactly the same way every time the behavior occurs (including mannerisms, tone of voice, and so on) and ensure that other significant adults in the child's life are doing the same.

5. Rewards are small and frequent.

Small, frequent rewards tend to work better than promises of large rewards in the distant future. Remember that for young children, anything more than a week seems like the distant future.

Family interactions can affect these systems. Disagreements among family members about a system cause inconsistency and reduce the system's effectiveness. Similarly, arguments with the child about whether or not a sticker is to be awarded reinforce arguing and reduce the system's effectiveness. Some parents even remove a sticker as a penalty for arguing. Regardless of the system used, all children benefit from sincere parental praise and from the intrinsic satisfaction of a job well done.

Benefits of Incentives

Incentive systems for children that emphasize the consequences of positive behavior boost self-esteem. They also avoid the problem of paying excessive attention to negative behaviors, which can inadvertently encourage those behaviors. All forms of attention can be perceived by children as something pleasant, causing negative behaviors to increase with attention.

Further, children who have displayed behaviors that are frustrating to their parents over a prolonged period are likely to have some feelings of being "bad." Emphasis on rewarding positive behavior instead of punishing negative behavior reduces the risk of further damage to their self-esteem.

Incentive systems can provide another benefit: They can reduce the incidence of family arguments. Because the rules of the system are clear to everyone, family interactions around behavior become more matter-of-fact and less emotionally charged. If the child performs the desired behavior, a small reward is provided. If the child does not perform the desired behavior, no reward is provided. Those are the rules. There is no need for angry or punitive interactions around the behavior. A few children will have a temper tantrum the first one or two times no reward is obtained, but as long as parents remain calm and persevere with their system, these children soon accept the rules.

9

QUESTIONS ABOUT INCENTIVE SYSTEMS

Isn't anxiety a feeling? Why are you emphasizing behavior?

Anxiety consists of a feeling, a way of thinking, a group of physical sensations, and a set of behaviors. Feelings, thought processes, and even physical sensations can change over a period of time, but behavior can change quickly. Thus, behavior management offers the hope of seeing results quickly, which is encouraging to both anxious children and their parents. Also, remember that prolonged avoidance of what is feared makes the fear worse, and the risk of such prolonged avoidance is reduced when behavioral measures are combined with a desensitization program.

Often, changing the behavior also influences feelings. Think how good it feels to accomplish something after a hard struggle. This is how an anxious child feels after mastering a previously avoided situation. Just as feelings affect behaviors, so too can behaviors affect feelings.

I don't think it's right to bribe a child with rewards. Won't the child get spoiled?

In helping sensitive children, rewards are used to promote exposure to feared situations. If the child does not face what is feared, there is no reward. Thus, the child learns that rewards are earned by doing something difficult, much as adults earn money for going to work each day. The child does *not* learn that the world will provide endless rewards, as feared by the parent who worries about spoiling. A bribe is a payment to induce someone to commit an illegal act. In contrast, a reward is compensation earned for a job well done. There is nothing illegal or devious about rewards.

My child keeps asking for expensive rewards. How can I afford this?

Because small, frequent rewards are more effective than large, infrequent ones, avoid really expensive items. Some children can be quite materialistic, even at an early age. Give a price range for the reward, and allow the child to choose something within that range. Alternatively, time and attention make excellent rewards. A trip to the movies with you can be just as reinforcing as an expensive toy. Other children prefer to earn television or computer time. Older children sometimes prefer using the incentive system to earn an extra dollar or two for their allowance. If your child is a collector (of stamps, baseball cards, bottle caps, and so forth), adding missing items to the collection can be very rewarding.

What if my child constantly worries about not getting her reward?

There are some anxious children who become preoccupied with their ability to earn rewards, to the point where the reward system actually increases anxiety. Often perfectionistic, these children may be overly self-conscious and worried about their performance on tasks, including the task being rewarded. If you see this happening to your child, stop using a formal reward system with charts and stickers. Instead, provide gentle praise and encouragement whenever the child makes progress to minimize self-consciousness. In extreme cases, parents sometimes have to avoid commenting on the behavior altogether, and instead find other ways to interact positively with their child.

What if the child can't control the fearful behavior?

When fears are accompanied by physical reactions such as vomiting, panic attacks, or stomachaches, the child may not be able to control the reaction. The child can still learn to cope, however, by handling that reaction more independently. In this case, reinforce independent handling of the problem.

Nancy hated bedtime. The thought of being alone in a dark room was scary, especially since she had become sick at her aunt's house a few months ago while her mom was away at a party. Every evening, the awful feeling in her stomach came back and she had to vomit. She called her mother in desperation as soon as she could feel it was about to happen and clung to her afterward for an hour or more before sleeping. The whole procedure took about two hours. Her mother was getting increasingly frustrated and tried to angrily pry her daughter away from her body after the vomiting. This only made Nancy cling harder.

A plan was worked out to help Nancy gradually learn to handle bedtime. Because the time after she vomited was hardest for Nancy, her ability to limit contact with her mother before she vomited was reinforced first. Soon, she was able to go to the bathroom by herself to vomit before calling her mother. Her mother responded reliably and was relieved that at least the procedure had been shortened to about one hour. As her anger decreased, she was able to reassure Nancy more quickly, and Nancy fell asleep easily in a few minutes. Nancy's nightly vomiting continued for a couple of months more before resolving, but she handled it with very little disruption to her family.

Do you keep reinforcing the behavior forever? Will the child ever learn to do it without a reward?

Once a behavior has been performed consistently for about three weeks, it is usually no longer challenging. At this point, most parents will substitute another desired behavior on the star chart. There is also a natural tendency in families for star charts to be forgotten or used only intermittently once the behavior is no longer a big deal. Continue to consistently praise the child's efforts, and go back to the chart if a relapse occurs. More families run into difficulty by stopping the reinforcements too soon (often when the child has performed the behavior only once or twice and is still struggling) than by continuing them for too long.

Also, try to gradually shift the emphasis from parental reinforcement to self-reinforcement by the child. Begin by modeling how you reinforce yourself. For example, when you finish a home-renovation project, think out loud about what aspects make you proud of the job.

Next, help the child to evaluate progress. In facing a feared situation, what did the child do that worked well? What could be done to make it even better next time? Always help the child find at least one positive aspect of what occurred. Remember, even an attempt to face what is feared is better than nothing. As the child learns, you can move from specific questions about what went well or not so well to more general questions such as "How did it go?" The goal is to eventually allow children to independently give themselves a pat on the back for facing fears.

Thus, a nice progression can occur from concrete rewards to parental praise to the child using self-evaluation and self-reward. Discussing the reasons for success also encourages children to attribute success to their own actions, rather than to good luck or to someone else's actions. Most successful adults have this attribution style.

10

DEFIANT BEHAVIOR AND DISINCENTIVES

L ike all children, sensitive children occasionally defy their parents. They may talk back, repeatedly respond to requests by arguing or saying no, insist things be done their way rather than yours, or even have temper tantrums. Defiance is part of most children's struggle to develop identities separate from their parents' and to feel they can have an impact on their environment. In fact, concern should arise when a child never refuses to do what you say.

Reasons for Defiant Behavior

Defiance can, however, become extreme in sensitive children who have a strong need to control every aspect of their environment. Where does this need come from? Recall that sensitive children are easily upset by change. Some have so little faith in their own ability to adapt to change that they try to stop it at all costs. They feel unsafe if people around them don't behave exactly according to their plans. They relax only when nothing changes and the environment is completely predictable. Unfortunately, this is unrealistic. Consequently, these children get into the habit of constantly struggling to make other people do things their way so that they will never be forced to deal with change. In the process, they behave very defiantly.

How can you tell if the child is defiant because of a fear of change or is just misbehaving? You can't. Fortunately, it doesn't matter. When you are trying to modify your child's behavior, there are only two kinds of behavior: desirable behavior and undesirable behavior. Defiance is generally undesirable.

Managing Defiant Behavior

If the defiance is minor, it is usually best to deliberately ignore it in order to avoid inadvertently encouraging it (recall that any attention from you encourages the behavior to continue).

If the defiance is more disruptive, withdraw something pleasant (for example, withdraw attention by placing the child in his room for a brief time-out) or administer something unpleasant (for example, remove television privileges that day or remove a dollar of allowance that week), consistent with the principles listed in Key 8 for dealing with undesirable behavior. Before adolescence, a time-out of about one minute per year of age (for example, five minutes for a five year old or ten minutes for a ten year old) can be highly effective. Losing allowance money is often more meaningful to a teenager.

This may seem like harsh treatment for the child whose defiant behavior is related to anxiety, but such behavior is not socially acceptable and must therefore be discouraged. Remember that people outside your home are unlikely to respond sympathetically to a child who is throwing a tantrum. Also, by stopping the defiant behavior and not doing what the child wants, you are forcing the child to face what is feared (for example, change in the environment). In the long run, this helps your child become less sensitive to change.

For children who display frequent defiant behavior, many parents use the "One, two, three" approach. This approach was first described by Thomas Phelan, Ph.D., who explains it in detail in his book *1-2-3 Magic* (see resource list). Briefly, the key is to warn the child who is continuing to misbehave by saying in a firm but emotionally neutral voice, "One" *and nothing else*, then "Two" *and nothing else*, and finally "That's Three. Take a five-minute time-out to your room." No discussion occurs, and failure to go to the room results in a suitable penalty (for example, a dollar less allowance). Used consistently, this approach has been found to be highly effective within about three weeks.

As with all disincentives, it is essential that it be administered with a minimum of talking and a minimum of emotion on the parent's part. Talking and emotion usually result in an escalation of the undesired behavior by providing the child with attention for it.

Occasionally, an anxious child may fear staying alone in a room. In this case, choose a different location, one where the child can serve time-out without feeling frightened (for example, in the corner or on the stairs), and apply the same system. Because you may be able to see the child during time-out, beware of allowing any verbal interaction to develop, as this defeats the purpose of time-out.

Some children are generally not defiant but have explosive outbursts in response to minor changes in their environment or situations they believe are unfair. They are often quite remorseful afterwards but have difficulty controlling this behavior. In these children, it is sometimes more helpful to assist them in anticipating the change or problem-solving the unfair situation than to provide repeated consequences or time-outs. Dr. Ross Greene has described this approach further in his book *The Explosive Child* (see resource list).

11

THE CHILD WHO WORRIES

Some children spend much of their time worrying. They pick up on every frightening event in the newspaper, in a book, or on television and relate it to themselves. Once they start worrying about something, they can't seem to stop. Rather than putting the frightening event in perspective and letting it go, they often go to their parents with a series of "What if?" questions.

> Child: What if burglars break into our house?
> Parent: It's not going to happen. The doors are locked.
> Child: But what if it does?
> Parent: We'll call the police.
> Child: But what if the burglars cut the telephone line?
> Parent: The dog will scare them off.
> Child: But what if they kill the dog?
> Parent: It's not going to happen, OK?
> Child: But what if . . .
> Parent: Stop this! You're being ridiculous!

At this point, the parent is feeling extremely frustrated about being unable to reassure the child and is also starting to get angry with the child. Hearing the angry tone of voice, the child feels even more frightened and responds by asking even more imploring questions. As the interaction between parent and child becomes more and more emotional, the parent feels trapped and increasingly helpless in dealing with the child. Some parents even admit that they must leave the situation at this point to avoid hitting the child in desperation.

It is important to remember, though, that children who approach their parents with worries are not trying to be deliberately frustrating.

How Worried Children Think

Worried children think differently from the way the average child thinks. They seem to have a kind of radar for danger, perceiving it everywhere and remembering only the most frightening and upsetting aspects of many situations. Researchers have found that worriers of all ages show this selective memory for what is frightening. In addition, they tend to underestimate their own ability to cope with situations, resulting in even greater fear. Finally, most of the time they don't live in the present. Their focus is either on reviewing past (perceived) failures in themselves or on anticipating potential disasters in the future. Worries prevent them from enjoying or even paying attention to many events happening around them at the moment. Extreme worrying in children is called *Generalized Anxiety Disorder*.

Some of these children will not acknowledge worrying, even though they look tense. In younger children, this may result from not understanding the concept of what a worry is. Other children, instead of discussing worries, may complain of physical symptoms in anticipation of feared events. For example, tense muscles may cause them to complain of stomachaches or headaches just before a test at school. They may also have trouble sleeping the night before a test. If this happens frequently, the child may become tired, cranky, and irritable much of the time. Finally, preoccupation with worries and lack of sleep can make it hard for these children to concentrate, to the point where they are sometimes mistakenly thought to have problems with attention. Boys who worry are especially prone to being mislabeled as having Attention Deficit Disorder, when instead their concentration problems may be more related to anxiety.

Curiously, it is the anticipation of a dreaded event, such as a test, that induces the most symptoms. Once the child is actually taking the test, the symptoms subside. The child is finally able to do something about the worry, and this action decreases the feeling of helplessness. Also, the test usually isn't nearly so bad as the child has previously imagined.

Distraction
Children can be helped to worry less. Many parents distract their child from worrying by encouraging the child to participate in a favorite activity, read an interesting book, or watch an enjoyable television show. This often works temporarily and comes in handy if you really don't have the time to deal with the child's worries on the spot. Many children eventually devise their own distractions. In the long run, however, worries are just like fears: They need to be faced and mastered if the child is to become less sensitive to them.

Identifying Worried Thinking
To master worries, children need to think differently. The distorted, worried thinking described above needs to be replaced with something more adaptive and more realistic. Before teaching this new thinking style to children, however, it is worth looking at the ways all of us sometimes distort our thinking to make life seem more frightening or more depressing than it really is. The following list describes such distortions of thinking.

Common Cognitive Distortions*

1. *Arbitrary inference.* The process of forming an interpretation of situations, events, or experiences when no factual evidence exists to support the conclusion or when the conclusion is contrary to evidence. For example, Jane thinks "Suzy didn't say hello to me this morning, so she must hate me," even though Suzy has been very friendly in the past and has shown no other signs of hatred or dislike.

2. *Selective abstraction.* The process of focusing on a (usually negative) detail taken out of context, ignoring other, more salient features of the situation. For example, a public speaker receives thunderous applause but sees one person in the audience napping and thinks the speech was poorly presented.

3. *Overgeneralization.* The process of drawing a general conclusion on the basis of a single incident. For example, Tommy strikes out once in a baseball game and concludes "I'm no good at baseball."

4. *Minimization or magnification.* The process of gross underestimation of events (such as one's performance, achievement, or ability) or of gross exaggeration (usually of an event perceived as traumatic) in which the person dwells on the worst possible outcome of a situation. For example, Mary (who fears dogs) thinks, "The streets are full of vicious dogs [magnification of danger] and there's nothing I can do to protect myself [minimizing own ability]."

5. *Dichotomous thinking* A tendency to interpret things in absolute, black-and-white terms, with little or no tolerance for uncertainty or ambiguity. For example, Ben thinks, "Becky took my side in the argument, and Linda

*Sources: A. T. Beck and G. Emery, *Anxiety Disorders and Phobias: A Cognitive Perspective* (New York: Basic Books, 1985), and M. McKay, M. Davis, and P. Fanning, *Thoughts and Feelings: The Art of Cognitive Stress Intervention* (Richmond, Calif.: New Harbinger Publications, 1981).

didn't; therefore, Becky is a good friend and Linda is not." In this case, Becky's faults and Linda's good qualities are conveniently ignored.

6. *Personalization.* The unsupported perception that an event reflects upon yourself (that is, taking things too personally). For example, you hear someone behind you laughing and assume the person is laughing at your appearance.

7. *Emotional reasoning.* Equating feelings with facts. A common example in depressed individuals is the thought "I feel like a loser, so I must be a loser." Anxious people commonly think, "I feel nervous in this situation, so I can't handle the situation."

Some Variations Common in Children and Adolescents

1. *Control fallacies.* The belief that others are responsible for your problems or that you are responsible for their problems. For example, Robert hears his parents arguing and assumes it is his fault.

2. *The fallacy of fairness.* The belief that what you want is the only thing that is fair. For example, George, who is a year older than his sister, tells his mother, "I'm older. I shouldn't have to go to bed at the same time she does. It's not fair!"

3. *The fallacy of change.* The belief that another person must be (or can be) pressured to change so that you can be happy. For example, Judy believes, "I have to make the teacher give me my test results today (rather than tomorrow when she'll give them to the rest of the class), so I can relax and sleep tonight."

4. *"Shoulds" fallacies.* Inflexible personal rules and expectations that are usually believed to be absolute in all situations and that include the words *should, ought,* or *must.* For example, "People should always return items they borrow on time and should do so without needing to be reminded."

If you find it difficult to remember all of these distortions, that's not unusual. It may help to think of them as relating to three aspects of life: personal competence, safety, and the future. Anxious people of all ages typically underestimate their own competence. They assume they are helpless and unable to cope with a situation when they may not be. At the same time, they typically overestimate the risks present in the world, so they feel unsafe in many situations even when this is not warranted. Finally, they may be preoccupied with the possibility of future disasters, assuming that if there is any uncertainty about what will happen in a situation, it will turn out badly. In summary, they generally see themselves as helpless to cope in an unsafe world where danger lurks just around the next corner.

Imagine how you would feel if you thought this way all the time. Imagine how a child feels who thinks this way all the time. This may be your anxious child's experience. To help, start by trying to recognize anxious thoughts in yourself. Most people use them automatically and are not even aware they are doing so. In fact, some people protest that they don't have such thoughts. Perhaps it is easier to think of these as biases rather than thoughts. The next time you feel even a little bit worried or tense, try to write down exactly what thought or bias is producing the tension. Chances are, what you write will contain one or more of the distortions listed. Most people who develop an awareness of these "automatic thoughts" can catch themselves using one at least once a day. People who suffer from more serious anxiety or depression use them all the time.

Next, try to find rational arguments to put the distorted thought in perspective. This may at first seem like a contrived game of "mental lawyer," but with practice this method of perspective taking becomes easier and seems more natural. Besides, it is difficult to get your child to think this way if you don't think this way yourself. Because it involves an internal dialogue with yourself, this technique is called *coping self-talk*.

Modeling Coping Thoughts

Modeling this new way of thinking is a very effective way of encouraging your child to use it. As many experienced parents have noted, children won't always do as you say but usually will do as you do. If you can say out loud some of the thoughts you use to reassure yourself, your child is likely to start thinking along similar lines.

> "I'm worried about this presentation at work tomorrow, but I'll probably do OK. After all, I've given many presentations successfully before, and some of those were longer than this one. Besides, I know a lot of the people who'll come to the presentation and they aren't all that critical. In fact, they'll probably be glad they don't have to be in the spotlight like me!"

If this feels artificial, try starting with some situations that lend themselves more naturally to coping talk. For example, suppose you are driving the family home from an outing and get caught in a snowstorm. You can assume that most children will be somewhat anxious in this situation, so it makes perfect sense to say "Oh, oh. We got caught in the snow. We've got snow tires, though, so we should be OK. If it gets really bad we can always get off the highway at the next exit and wait till the weather clears up."

Modeling is especially useful for those anxious children who completely refuse to talk about their fears, even with the most sensitive, encouraging parent. They may feel embarrassed about the fear or feel anxious about even having to think about it. Anxiety also tightens the vocal cords and dries the mouth, making it physically harder to talk. Regardless of the reason for the silence, these children still listen and observe others. Some of these children learn to cope by observation alone, without ever acknowledging their parents' influence.

12

HELPING WORRIED CHILDREN COPE

Despite your best efforts to model realistic thinking for your child, you may still be approached with worries and "What if?" questions from time to time. The tendency for sensitive children to focus on the most frightening aspects of situations does not change overnight. This Key presents a method for reassuring children who express worries to you, and the next Key describes how to gradually allow children to assume responsibility for reassuring themselves.

A typical situation that induces worries in a sensitive child: Suppose your child's teacher gets up on the wrong side of the bed and shouts at the child for talking out of turn.

The average child thinks, "Ms. Smith sure is crabby. Better stay out of her way today."

The anxious child thinks, "Oh, no. She yelled, so she must hate me. She'll probably fail me. I'll fail and never succeed at school again! My life is over!"

The anxious child who has learned coping self-talk thinks, "There are lots of reasons for Ms. Smith to yell besides hating me. Even if she does, so what? She can't kill me. The worst she can do is lower my mark. Even if she does that I probably won't fail, because I've passed all her tests so far. Besides, there are other teachers who like me and will give me better marks. No point getting all upset. Let's see what else is going on in class today."

How do you convince your child to think this way? You don't. Anxious children are almost impossible to convince. However, you can help your child by challenging the reality of worries and thus aiding the development of coping self-talk. Coping self-talk is based on a realistic appraisal of the frightening situation, not just naive positive thinking. People who cope well take an experimental approach to life. If a situation is frightening, they do a "reality check" by asking themselves, "Is this fear or worry about a real danger or is it related to anxiety?" If they're not sure, they check it out. If it's a realistic fear, they do something about it. If it's not realistic, they acknowledge their anxiety and use coping self-talk to reduce it. Helping your child test reality also shows that you are taking his or her feelings seriously and that you are willing to join in the struggle to deal with them.

If a child says there's a ghost in the closet, don't argue. Open the closet to check it out.

If a child sees a neighbor's house burn down and subsequently becomes terrified of the possibility of a house fire, make sure the fear is unrealistic. Telling the child about the low probability of two house fires on the same street is not very convincing if your smoke detector is broken.

Labeling the Anxiety

Suppose you have challenged the reality of your child's worries and it is clear to both you and the child that the fear is unrealistic.

Find a name for this uncomfortable feeling the child is experiencing as a result of unrealistic fear. Whether you call it anxiety, nerves, fear, stress, or "that queasy feeling" really doesn't matter. Avoid an insulting (and untrue) label like "it's all in your head." The important thing is to choose a name that is acceptable to the child and that the two of you can talk about. Young children often do better if you personify the problem. Call it "the fear bully" or "the scaredy bear," for example. Having a name for anxiety makes it seem more concrete and manageable to the child.

Giving the feeling a name also helps to externalize anxiety. Anxious children often feel very bad about themselves, to the point where they think, "I *am* a problem" rather than "I *have* a problem." Giving anxiety a name emphasizes the distinction between the child and the problem. Once an anxious child knows "There's more to me than my anxiety," that child becomes more motivated and hopeful about beating the problem. This way of thinking also results in your seeing more of your child's strengths, allowing you to team up with your child against the problem rather than becoming angry and blaming the child.

Furthermore, you can use the name to help your child learn to recognize anxiety. Just like adults, many children have anxious thoughts, feelings, or physical sensations without realizing these are caused by anxiety.

An anxious child may breathe very quickly the morning she is supposed to start going to a new school. She doesn't realize she's anxious, but she feels dizzy and nauseated and complains of a pins-and-needles sensation in her hands. All the symptoms are caused by breathing too quickly (also called hyperventilation). Helping her recognize that this is anxiety rather than some strange new disease may be quite reassuring, especially if she has already learned some skills for dealing with anxiety. The disappearance of her symptoms when you help her slow down her breathing should provide further reassurance.

Providing the Child with the Facts About Anxiety

The following facts about anxiety may be reassuring:

1. Nobody's ever died from it.
2. It always goes away (the body runs out of adrenaline).

3. It doesn't mean you're crazy. Everybody has it some-times.

4. Not sleeping for a night, not eating for a day, or other changes in routine occurring because of this feeling are not fatal either. (One exception: not drinking fluids for days, but this is rare and not worth mentioning to the child.)

Learning Coping Self-Talk

Once you have given the anxiety a name, the child can then begin to learn coping self-talk.

Most coping self-talk for worried children is based on four questions:

1. How likely is it that what I'm afraid of will actually happen/has actually happened? (Remembering that if it's never or only rarely happened before, the chances are slim.)

2. What other explanations are there for this situation besides the one I'm worried about?

3. Even if the worst should happen, would it be so bad? How could I handle it?

4. Is there anything I can do about the situation? If not, what can I do to take my mind off the worries?

The answers to these questions can be quite reassuring as shown in the example of coping with Ms. Smith's yelling.

The four questions can be reduced to two, more general ones:

1. What can I *think about* to reduce my anxiety? (Questions 1–3 above.)

2. What can I *do* to reduce my anxiety? (Question 4 above.)

Relaxation techniques and activities that distract from worries can be used to address the question of what to do and are described in Keys 14 and 15.

If your child still has difficulty coping even though you have made a concerted effort to use the approach in this Key, a particular form of psychotherapy may be helpful. Cognitive behavioral therapy (abbreviated CBT) can help anxious children cope using techniques similar to those described here. That is, it helps children change their anxiety-related thoughts (called *anxious cognitions*) and reduce the tendency to avoid anxiety-provoking situations (called *anxious behavior* or *avoidant behavior*).

Dr. Philip Kendall, who pioneered this work, uses a four-step plan based on the acronym FEAR. Each letter stands for a step in this plan, which is described in Key 13. Children learn the FEAR plan and then apply it to a variety of anxiety-provoking situations, beginning with easy ones and working up to more challenging ones. Eventually, it becomes routine, increasing the child's confidence and thus reducing anxious avoidance of what is feared. Studies in numerous countries have now demonstrated the benefits of this type of CBT for anxious children when provided either individually or to a small group of similar-aged children.

Because this approach is challenging for some anxious children to master (for example, children with learning disabilities or with other mental health problems in addition to anxiety), newer adaptations of this work have recently been developed. For example, Dr. Bruce Chorpita has described a CBT approach for anxious children that he terms *modular* (see resource list). A module is a lesson focusing on one of the component skills of CBT. By breaking CBT into modules, it can be taught at a pace suitable to the individual child. Also, not every child may need every module, so the therapist has more flexibility in designing the treatment.

13

GETTING CHILDREN TO COPE ALONE

Because you cannot always be there to help your worried child cope, it is important to get the child to eventually use this approach routinely, regardless of your presence or absence. Getting your child to cope alone is not easy. The following is a description of what not to do when conveying a coping approach to your child.

If you want to turn your child off this approach completely, start by having the child sit in front of you while you deliver a lecture on coping self-talk. Then, don't let the child leave the room until all four coping questions have been committed to memory. Finally, expect the child to regularly use coping self-talk with no reminders or further involvement on your part. Teaching coping self-talk this way is almost universally unsuccessful.

Gradually Coping More Independently

To get children to cope on their own, use a gradual approach based on small steps, just as you did earlier for facing fears. Suppose your child is anxious, you have named the feeling and are talking about it, and you have modeled coping self-talk previously. Begin asking the child one or two of the four specific coping questions. Use the ones you think would be most reassuring for that particular fear or worry. Make a game of it, if you can. If an anxious child has a bruise and reads in a medical book that bruising can be a sign of cancer, challenge the child to find as many other reasons as possible for having a bruise. Repeat this process each time your child experiences anxiety in your presence or tells you about an anxiety-provoking situation. Don't insist that your child use the questions verbatim. Some children will find their own words for the questions. For example, rather than thinking about "alternative explanations for a situation," the child may think, "What are some excuses for Mom being late?"

Try to avoid giving the child the answers without first asking the questions. Most people learn best when they are actively involved in the process, rather than just passively receiving information. Having to think about the questions gets your child involved. Thinking also distracts your child from anxiety. Finally, coming up with the answers on their own gives children a sense of mastery that builds up their confidence.

Eventually, the questions become second nature. At this point, the child may remember the specific questions if you provide the two more general ones to get started. Further on, your child may only need you to label the anxiety in order to begin using coping self-talk. Finally, the child will use coping self-talk independently, with only an occasional reminder.

Remember that your child will be able to think most clearly when only mildly anxious. Once your child is experiencing panic or severe anxiety, all forms of logical reasoning (including coping self-talk) become impossible. *Highly anxious children cannot think clearly, so stop talking and offer comfort.* Reassure your child that the anxiety will pass, and encourage taking a few deep breaths; then, once the child is calm, you can talk about coping.

A Handy Memory Aid
How do you get your child to remember all this? Once you have established that there is no realistic basis for your child's

fear, the mnemonic *FEAR* works nicely as a reminder of what to do when anxious. It was first developed by Philip Kendall, Ph.D., at Temple University.

F = This is *F*ear (or stress, nerves, queasiness, and so forth), nothing else. (Labeling the anxiety.)

E = What do I *E*xpect to happen? (Asking self the four questions; coping self-talk. Some children prefer: What do I say to *E*nd the worries?)

A = What *A*ction can I take to get through this? (Relaxation; distracting activity. See Keys 14 and 15.)

R = Hurray! I got through it. Time for a *R*eward. (See Keys 8 and 9 for a discussion of rewards/incentives.)

Have the child make a decorative "FEAR card." By keeping this card in a coat pocket, the child can use it as a helpful memory aid whenever it is needed. The card may also provide reassurance for the child when anxious away from home.

If talking about the fears makes your child anxious or otherwise upset, this approach is still worth trying. When people walk on eggshells to avoid mentioning their child's fears, they are supporting the child's avoidance of what is feared. This doesn't help the child. When a child talks about what is feared (or hears parents talking about it), that child is mentally facing the fear. This is the first step toward desensitization and decreased worry.

The Younger Child

Correcting worried thinking works best for children who are at least seven years old, but it can be modified for younger children. Reality testing works in young and old alike. As described, the name you choose for anxiety may be simpler or more concrete for the younger child. Most young children can understand basic emotions if they are labeled "sad," "mad," "glad," and "scared." Alternatively, you may want to draw a face with an open mouth and raised eyebrows as a symbol of fear. A relaxed, "glad" face can be drawn in contrast to the "scared" one. A nice way to model coping in young children is to read them a story in which a character copes with fear. The *Annie Stories* book included in the resource list may be helpful. Having the child pretend to be a brave storybook character can also be useful in learning coping self-talk. A variation on this is to role-play a frightened character yourself and have the child role-play a brave one who is teaching your character how to be brave. It is surprising how well some anxious children cope when allowed to pretend that they are an authority on the subject.

Joey was worried about going to kindergarten. He had gone before, but cried and carried on terribly each time. Joey didn't have a large vocabulary, and he didn't like answering questions. He did enjoy hearing stories and liked to play pretend. Two of his favorite characters were a frightened cat and a heroic tiger. Whenever Joey was frightened, he was asked, "What would Joey Scaredy-Cat say?" and then, "What would Joey the Tiger say?" He quickly mastered coping self-talk.

Young children can also learn simple breathing exercises. Further, these children tend to respond to rewards more quickly than older children do. Key 22 provides further suggestions for helping children of different ages with their anxieties.

Preparing for Stressful Events

If your child worries about stressful events days or even weeks in advance, you don't necessarily have to do weeks of coping self-talk. Some parents of children who worry a great deal in anticipation of events choose not to mention the event until shortly before it happens or even after the fact (for example, if a favorite relative is having an operation). They usually do this when they doubt that the child, if informed earlier, will be able to cope with the event. This approach is a compromise, since it reduces your child's time for doing coping self-talk for the sake of reducing worrying time. It does work for some children, however, especially in the case of very frightening situations. Ultimately, you have to make a judgment call about what you think your child can handle.

If you opt for trying the coping self-talk, go back to the principles described above: Is the worry realistic? If there is something your child can do to prepare for the event, make sure the child does it. There is no point in telling a child not to worry about a test if the child hasn't studied adequately. Similarly, a child can't stop worrying about a presentation if the child hasn't rehearsed for it. Even if nothing can be done at that moment, getting your child to write down how to cope on the day of the event can be helpful.

Then, remind your child that everything that can be done to prepare has been done. The rest is beyond the child's control. This may sound frightening at first, because anxious children often reassure themselves by trying to control everything in their environment. It is important, however, to help your child learn that worrying does not increase control; it only increases anxiety. Once all that can be done has been done, the rest is determined by fate (or God, providence, and so on, depending on one's beliefs), regardless of whether or not one worries. Because worrying increases anxiety, at this point it is worth trying some of the relaxation techniques from the next Key.

14

RELIEVING
PHYSICAL STRESS

Many children who worry or have fears also suffer the physical symptoms of stress (for example, headaches, stomachaches, or hyperventilating). The approach to coping described so far, however, has emphasized thoughts and self-talk. These techniques do not always relieve physical stress. Also, children who are not very verbal may have some difficulty applying coping self-talk. Such children may find it more helpful to learn how to take *action* when they are frightened. Even those children who use self-talk effectively can benefit from such anxiety-reducing actions.

The practice of relaxation is the most basic anxiety-reducing action. This sounds like a simple topic. After all, everyone knows how to relax, right? Try an experiment. The next time someone you care about looks stressed, order that person to relax. What happens? The next time you can't sleep at night, tell yourself to "just relax." What happens?

Unfortunately, relaxation is not so simple. Most people become relaxed in certain circumstances (for example, lying on the beach while on vacation), but the ability to relax in daily life must be learned and takes some practice. Like anxiety, relaxation has physical, mental, and emotional aspects. Being physically inactive in front of the television, for example, is *not* a good way of clearing your mind of worries or calming distressing feelings.

You will recall that the fight-or-flight response prepares the body for handling dangerous situations. This response is triggered by the sympathetic nervous system. Opposing this response is the parasympathetic nervous system, which triggers the body's natural relaxation response. These two systems compete, and people feel more or less anxious depending on which one is dominant at any given time. People cannot force themselves to relax. The techniques described in this Key, however, can make it *more likely* that the parasympathetic nervous system (relaxation response) will be switched on instead of the sympathetic nervous system (fight-or-flight response). Children are far more likely to use these techniques if someone else in the family does them as well. Say "Let's do our relaxation" rather than "Do your relaxation now," and your child will probably be more motivated to try.

Abdominal Breathing

The basic relaxation technique of abdominal breathing can be learned by children of almost all ages, especially if an adult practices with the child. Have the child sit up (no slouching) but in a comfortable position, wearing loose clothing. Watch his breathing pattern. Next, encourage the child to count to four slowly each time he breathes in, then exhale. Watch the shoulders. If they are rising, challenge the child to continue breathing slowly without raising the shoulders. Make a game of it. Now, have the child put his hand on his belt (or belly button) and try to push out the belt each time he inhales. This is abdominal breathing.

The idea is to force air slowly into the base of the lungs. This stretches the diaphragm, a muscle at the base of the lungs. The nerves attached to the diaphragm trigger the body's natural relaxation response. Most meditation techniques use this style of breathing, as do trained singers, martial arts instructors, and some athletes. It takes about 20 minutes of practice per day to learn this technique. Many children find this is easiest to do just before going to bed, when relaxation aids sleep. After three or four weeks of daily practice, most children develop the ability to use this technique as needed when tense during the day.

Remember to keep it slow. Fast, deep breathing is hyperventilation and actually *produces* anxiety symptoms such as faintness, dizziness, and tingling of the hands. If the child breathes too quickly, have him mentally say "One, Mississippi, two Mississippi, three Mississippi, four Mississippi, exhale" with each breath. Some children need a count of five or even six to slow down. Inhaling and holding the breath for a count of three is an alternative method for slowing down. Children who can't stop raising their shoulders may find it helpful to be told to "breathe like a puppy dog" (fast, shallow panting) and then to do the opposite. To encourage use of the diaphragm, suggest the child "blow up the tummy like a balloon."

Progressive Muscle Relaxation

Progressive muscle relaxation is another simple technique often used to trigger relaxation. Have the child lie down or sit up comfortably, again wearing loose clothing. Start with the fingers and ask the child to scrunch them up as tight as possible . . . then relax them. Next, make two fists as tight as possible . . . then relax them. Continue working toward the center of the body, one muscle group at a time. Remember that the face and jaw also have muscles that are often tense. It is easier if you use a professional recording or make a recording of your own voice (see next section) so that you don't get too preoccupied with whether or not all the muscle groups were covered. The idea is to have the child learn to distinguish between the tense and relaxed states so that, eventually, the muscles can be relaxed voluntarily without having to tense them first. Again, this takes some practice.

Relaxation Recordings

Obtain a relaxation recording (tape, CD, or MP3) that, for a good 20 minutes, talks you through abdominal breathing and/or progressive muscle relaxation. Try the recording yourself first, to decide if it is appropriate for your child. Alternatively, make your own spoken recording, using the information in this Key and perhaps some soft background music. Once you have an appropriate tape, listen to it with the child. Try having the child teach you how to do the exercise. Acting the part of the expert boosts the confidence of many worried children. Recordings are also helpful in encouraging the child's independent handling of anxiety, as the child can use them without a parent's help.

Physical Versus Psychological Pain

"But the pain is real. It's not in my head!" many children will protest. These children have difficulty connecting physical symptoms with emotional states. When you suggest an emotional cause, they feel hurt and misunderstood. They are unlikely to participate in any relaxation exercises you suggest until their hurt is acknowledged. Rather than getting into a debate about what's physical and what's psychological, express some empathy for the child's experience and focus on solutions. Once children realize that something can be done about the problem, they are far more likely to listen to an explanation of its causes. If they still insist it's physical, so what? If they can cope, the question of what caused the problem becomes academic. Remember, the stomach pain caused by muscle tension can be just as intense as that caused by an ulcer or other physical problem.

Ashley was convinced that her abdominal pain was caused by a serious illness. All the pediatrician's tests had come back normal, but Ashley didn't believe them. "The problem is my stomach, not my head" she asserted. Ashley had a number of family problems that had to be very anxiety-provoking for her, but arguing the point wouldn't help. Instead, she was asked to rate the severity of her pain. It was eight out of ten. She was then engaged in a discussion of some neutral topics—a school field trip she had mentioned, the ballet lessons she enjoyed, and so on. Ashley became involved in the conversation, started joking, and was no longer clutching her abdomen. After half an hour, she was asked, "By the way, how is the pain now?" To her surprise, it was only three out of ten. The therapist didn't comment (there's nothing worse for a child than an adult saying, "I told you so") but repeated the demonstration in a couple of subsequent sessions. Ashley never admitted to being anxious, but she did start using conversation with friends to take her mind off the stomach pain, which eventually resolved.

One caution: Even a very anxious child who frequently reports physical symptoms occasionally gets ill. It is tempting to ignore the child who often cries wolf, but to do so can be dangerous. Instead, look for an objective measure of illness. Taking the child's temperature is a good one for flulike symptoms. When in doubt, consult a physician.

15
RELAXING THE MIND

Settling worried thoughts can be more difficult than physical relaxation for some children. When they try to unwind at the end of the day, the result is often the opposite. During the day, the child is busy and doesn't have much time to worry. In the evening, the mind is free to wander, and it usually wanders to worries. Thus, although it may sound like a paradox, relaxing the mind actually involves getting the child to concentrate. When the mind has a focus, it can't worry.

Focusing the Mind

Several techniques can help focus a racing mind. For example, if your child is already doing a breathing exercise, have her concentrate on the air going in and out one nostril. Tell your child that whenever a worry or anxious thought comes up, she is to concentrate again on the air moving through that nostril. This approach can be learned more formally through mindfulness meditation tapes, which are appealing to older children and adolescents who have trouble "turning off the wheels of the mind" at bedtime. Dr. Jon Kabat-Zinn has produced a number of tapes focused on this technique (see resource list). Counting also provides a focus for the mind, hence the old suggestion to "count sheep" at bedtime. Some children find it helpful to focus on something particularly boring to get to sleep. One little girl reported "boring herself to sleep" by staring at the wall in her room.

Any mental task requiring concentration will focus the mind and thus interfere with worries. Some worriers read themselves to sleep or do crossword puzzles until they feel tired. The relaxing effect of concentration also explains the common observation that children who fear school are much more worried before going than after arriving and starting their work, as well as the fact that passively watching television is rarely relaxing.

Visualization

Visualizing something relaxing or fun often helps younger children take their minds off worry or pain. Encourage imagining the scene in detail with all its sights, sounds, feelings, smells, and tastes. It may help to add a reassuring character to the scene, such as a parent, friend, or storybook hero. For example, one little boy, while sitting in the dentist's chair, imagined himself going through the exhibits at Disneyland with his favorite television superhero. Meditation exercises for younger children also use imagery in anxiety-reducing ways. *Spinning Inward* (see resource list) is one book that describes such meditations.

Encouraging Your Child to Practice

Children can't be forced to do these exercises, only encouraged. Doing the exercises with the child and taking a lighthearted approach may increase the chances of the child cooperating. Another "selling point" for relaxation techniques is that they are unobtrusive. Thus, a child can use the techniques when anxious without anyone else having to know about it. This can be appealing for children who are embarrassed about their anxiety. If the child still refuses to participate, don't push it. It works better to invite children to try a variety of coping techniques and decide for themselves which ones work best than to get into a power struggle about any one technique. You may also wish to leave a relaxation tape in the child's room, because some children who resent being asked to do something by their parents will later do it on their own. Some children will not practice relaxation formally, but they enjoy activities that include some of these techniques. Yoga, for example, can be very relaxing and appealing to some children. Voice lessons teach diaphragmatic breathing, as do some forms of martial arts.

When helping your child relax, avoid strong negative emotions. Strong negative emotions, especially anger, will override any relaxation technique. It doesn't help to teach the child abdominal breathing or visualization if family arguments take place every evening. If an upset has occurred earlier in the day, talk about it to clear the air. Nobody relaxes or sleeps very well in the presence of unresolved hurt feelings.

When Anxiety Becomes Overwhelming

All these coping and relaxation techniques work best when anxiety is recognized early and is not yet severe. Most anxious children have some times when, despite your best efforts, they get overwhelmed. At that point, don't frantically search for more techniques. Instead, label the anxiety, have the child take a few slow breaths, and emphasize that the anxiety will soon pass. For some children, writing down the worries or drawing pictures of them can also be helpful. Other children respond better to a gentle hug. The worries can then be examined later, once the child has calmed down.

16

DIET, EXERCISE, AND SLEEP

Maintaining good physical health and regular routines often reduces a child's overall level of anxiety and enhances the child's ability to cope. This Key examines what is known about the effects of diet, exercise, and sleep on anxiety.

Diet

Caffeine is the only dietary substance consistently shown to increase anxiety. Caffeine should be avoided because it turns on the sympathetic nervous system, which is responsible for the fight-or-flight response. Thus, it induces the physical symptoms usually associated with anxiety (rapid heartbeat, rapid breathing, sweating, irritability, and so on). Feeling these symptoms often makes people worry and feel anxious. Caffeine is contained in coffee, tea, chocolate, cola beverages, and so-called energy drinks. Certain painkillers (for example, Excedrin and Anacin) and headache remedies may also contain caffeine.

Other substances that stimulate the sympathetic nervous system and thus increase anxiety are found in inhalers used for asthma, decongestants, and some cold remedies. Check with your pharmacist if you're not sure. Certain street drugs also contain stimulants (for example, cocaine) and should, of course, be avoided.

To date, there is no good evidence that any other dietary substances contribute to anxiety. Despite the folklore around sugar, food additives, and other substances that are said to make children "hyper," well-controlled studies have not shown any of these to affect anxiety one way or the other. Thus, the best recommendation is probably to eat a balanced diet containing the four major food groups (fruits and vegetables, breads and cereals, dairy products, and meat or other protein sources) and avoid caffeine products.

Anxious children are sometimes picky eaters, resulting in excessive concern about their food intake. If you are concerned, check with your pediatrician or family doctor. The doctor should have a record of your child's growth over the past several years, usually in the form of a graph. The graph will show your child's height and weight, compared with those of other children of the same age, at different times. If, when compared with other children, your child is still on the same growth curve as charted previously, you have nothing to be concerned about. If your child appears to be falling behind, however, discuss with your doctor how best to deal with the problem. Avoid power struggles with the child over food. These usually make the problem worse and can, in the long run, predispose the child to eating disorders. Leaving some nutritious snacks around the house is often an easy way to supplement the diet of a nibbler.

Conversely, some anxious children overeat, usually in an attempt to soothe feelings of tension. For these children, eating is no longer related to appetite alone. Instead, it becomes a nervous habit much like nail-biting or fidgeting. It is most likely to occur when the mind is not fully occupied, for example, while watching television. Limiting television time, limiting access to high-fat snacks, and helping the child find other ways of relieving tension all help. Other strategies are discussed in Key 28 on nervous habits. If the child is becoming increasingly obese, consult a physician and once again try to avoid power struggles over food.

Exercise

People sometimes wonder whether physical exercise may contribute to anxiety because it makes the heart beat faster. This rarely happens. In fact, regular exercise releases the body's natural painkillers, called *endorphins*, which contribute to relaxation. Exercise also makes children tired and thus improves sleep. Over time, aerobic exercise (exercise that makes the heart and lungs work hard) also results in a lower heart rate and in lower blood pressure. This may be beneficial, for studies have shown that anxious children, on average, have higher heart rates than their peers. Sports involving peers can also build confidence and social skills.

Occasionally, anxious children may be frightened when feeling their hearts beating with exertion. If this is interpreted as a normal physiological change that everyone experiences when exercising, most children are reassured. On balance, regular moderate exercise is helpful for most anxious children.

Sleep

Anxious children vary in how much sleep they need. Because of their anxiety, some children will find daily life quite stressful and thus require more sleep, especially once they begin facing their fears. Others seem to sleep less, commonly because of worries that interfere with getting to sleep. There is no absolute rule on how much sleep is needed. A good rule of thumb is that if the child is able to keep up at school and doesn't look overly tired, sleep is probably adequate.

To promote good sleeping habits, the following tips may be helpful:

- Have the child get up at the same time of day, regardless of bedtime.
- Discourage daytime napping.

- Make sure the child gets plenty of physical activity during the day, but not right before bedtime.
- Avoid cola, chocolate, tea, or any other caffeine-containing products in the evening.
- Avoid overly exciting activities in the evening.
- Use the bedroom primarily for sleep, and discourage eating or watching television in bed.
- Use warm milk with or without cereal to help sleep (milk contains a sleep-inducing substance called *tryptophan*).
- If the child can't get to sleep, suggest quietly doing another activity until tired.

Often, a bigger problem than sleep itself is the amount of concern in the child or in the family about not sleeping. Focusing excessively on sleep problems tends to make them worse. Getting the child to handle bedtime independently *whether or not* the child sleeps is often helpful. Also, reassure the child that the body will eventually catch up, even if there are some bad nights.

Physical Problems

Could your child have a physical problem that is causing the anxiety? Some medications and nonprescription remedies can have anxiety as a side effect. Check with your pharmacist or doctor if you are not sure.

Certain heart problems (such as mitral valve prolapse), thyroid problems, and other hormone problems have been associated with anxiety but do not necessarily cause it. One study found that children with inhibited temperament (a possible risk factor for anxiety) had a higher incidence of allergies and asthma than children without this trait. Again, this does not necessarily mean that allergies or asthma cause anxiety. When anxiety is associated with a physical problem, it is often unclear whether the physical problem has caused the anxiety, the anxiety is aggravating the physical problem, or some third factor is contributing to both the anxiety and the physical problem. In general, a thorough examination by a pediatrician can determine whether any significant physical problems may be affecting your child's anxiety level.

Dealing with a serious illness or disability can certainly exacerbate anxiety. Anxious children with physical disabilities often feel embarrassed or different. Meeting other children with similar disabilities can help the child feel less odd, and disabled children can often learn from each other how to better cope with people's reactions to them.

Anxious children requiring repeated hospitalizations often find these traumatic, especially if separated from their parents for extended periods. Even emergency room visits or visits to the doctor can be traumatic for children predisposed to anxiety. Many hospitals allow parents to "room in" with the hospitalized child, especially if the child is very young. Ask if this is possible, as it can be very reassuring for a young child. Regular parental visits and full explanations of medical procedures are often more reassuring for the older child.

17

CHANGE AND THE SENSITIVE CHILD

The one characteristic exhibited most consistently by sensitive children of all ages is difficulty adapting to change. The unpredictability of new situations increases the sensitive child's sense of personal vulnerability and fear of possible danger. Anxious children cope much better when the predictability of daily life is increased.

To make your child's life more predictable, try the following:

1. Have your child use the same routine every morning to get ready for school and every evening to get ready for bed. For example, suppose that in order to get ready for school your child must get up, go to the bathroom, get dressed, have breakfast, brush his teeth, collect his books, and walk to the bus stop. Get into the habit of having your child do these things in the same order and at approximately the same time every day. This consistency reassures the child that things are predictable and under control, while reassuring you that your child will get out the door on time.

2. Predictably say the same reassuring phrases to your anxious child. This practice improves the child's ability to cope and to face anxiety-provoking situations more quickly. As one parent put it, "I feel like a broken record, but it seems to work!"

3. Introduce your child to only one new situation at a time. For example, if you are planning a family outing to the zoo, it may not be wise to add on a trip to a relative's house afterward. Arriving at your destination a few minutes early to give your child a chance to adjust to the new surroundings may also be helpful.

   Similarly, when planning after-school activities, begin by enrolling the child in only one activity. Encourage the child to give it a try and then praise the child's attempts to do so. Wait until the child is clearly comfortable there before suggesting a second activity.

4. Help your child to plan ahead as a way of coping with change. A favorite technique is the "just in case" plan. This works best for children who already have some other coping skills but lack confidence in their own ability to use them. Parent and child work out a plan just in case the child feels overwhelmed. Examples would be thinking about where the nearest washroom is located, just in case the child panics at school, and carrying a quarter in a pocket, just in case the child feels the need to call home. Knowing that a contingency plan exists often helps the child relax to the point where the plan is rarely used.

   Planning *with* rather than *for* the child is usually more helpful. This encourages the child's independent thinking and thus, eventually, decreases reliance on the parent. Have the child come up with at least some of the ideas for handling a new situation, even if you have to leave clues. Help the child to evaluate the various options, using pros and cons. Finally, encourage choosing the ideas that make the most sense to the child. Be positive about the child's participation in the process, even if the option you think is best is not chosen. Over time, children using this approach feel far less helpless than those who are just told what to do. They are thus more likely to attempt to solve problems on their own.

Big Changes

For big changes, some rehearsal and collaboration with other people may be required. Most parents can anticipate situations where their child is very likely to feel overwhelmed. Going to a new school and going to overnight camp for the first time are typical examples.

Breaking down the "big event" into several little changes with the child and thinking of coping strategies for each can help.

For example, going to a new school typically involves

- Finding transportation to and from the new school and getting used to using it
- Meeting and interacting with unfamiliar children
- Meeting new teachers and getting used to their expectations
- Finding one's way around a new building
- Getting used to a new class schedule
- Dealing with new academic tasks at school
- Dealing with new homework tasks
- Sometimes, getting used to having lunch in a cafeteria
- Sometimes, getting used to after-class activities at the school

Looking at that list, no wonder the child is scared!

Most children, however, aren't worried about all of the above. Usually, there are one or two main concerns. Explore with the child which ones are most worrisome, and then put the worries in perspective (as described previously). Next, see if a little practice can be arranged during the summer break. Using public transportation to get to the new school is certainly amenable to practice. With a few telephone calls, you may also be able to arrange an advance meeting with the new teacher or a tour of the school building. See if any of your child's friends are going to the new school and, if so, suggest they go together, at least in the beginning.

Finally, remind the child that all the other new children will be in exactly the same position in September, but your child has the advantage of having prepared. There are still likely to be a few sleepless nights initially, but a change that might otherwise be experienced as traumatic is now merely a time of adjustment for your child.

The Senses

New sensory experiences can be particularly challenging for sensitive children. Unwillingness to wear certain clothes, extreme reactions to noise, and aversion to certain tastes or smells are commonly reported in sensitive children. Some of these sensitivities interfere very little in the child's life. In this case, you can either ignore them or adjust the child's environment for greater comfort. For example, if the child is upset when someone in the family plays the stereo at maximum volume, you may elect to just turn it down. That will preserve everyone's hearing. If the child's classroom is noisy, this can often be limited by placing old tennis balls on the bottoms of chair and table legs. Ear plugs may be useful for school assemblies or other particularly noisy situations.

Dealing with the child who refuses to wear all but two outfits can be a little more difficult. Some possible approaches include providing incentives for trying new outfits or disincentives for wearing the old ones (until the child desensitizes to the fabrics), allowing the child to wear one of the old outfits only after washing it (a natural consequence that allows the child to take responsibility for the problem), and doing nothing and waiting until ridicule by peers or other people prompts the child to change into other clothes (a more drastic natural consequence). Nagging or trying to physically force the child into other clothes tends to aggravate the problem.

Dealing with the Unexpected

Helping anxious children deal with the unexpected is not easy. Unexpected situations are among the most difficult ones for them to tolerate. Most people manage their anxiety, to a degree, by making life more predictable. Using a daily schedule is a common example of this approach. It is only when anxiety has been reduced to the point where life is starting to get boring that the unexpected becomes a welcome surprise. Anxious children are rarely in this state. The best parents can do is to help their anxious child recognize that unexpected events, though stressful, are not necessarily disastrous. "You got through it!" is often the most reassuring thing to say.

18

WHEN TO CONSIDER MEDICATION

Most sensitive children do not require medication; they overcome their fears and worries using the other coping methods described in this book. Nevertheless, some children do require medication, and people around them may have unusually strong feelings about this form of treatment. Just mentioning the word *medication* provokes fear and outrage in some parents and raises the magical promise of "cure" in others. Both are extreme reactions.

Medication is like any other treatment: Using it depends on assessing the balance of risks versus benefits for each individual child. Sometimes it is very beneficial, sometimes it changes little, and occasionally it causes further problems. The same could be said of psychotherapy, behavior modification, or any other form of treatment. Medication reduces symptoms of anxiety while it is in the body. Children who experience fewer anxiety symptoms are often able to function better and develop additional coping skills.

After awhile, the additional skills and confidence resulting from a child's improved functioning may reduce the amount of medication the child needs. In some cases, medication is eventually no longer required at all. In other cases, it continues to be required but at a low dose or only during unusually stressful times.

Medication may be useful in several ways:

1. *Making it easier for the child to face what is feared.* Medication reduces the child's anticipatory anxiety to the point where exposure to the feared situation seems much less threatening.

> Since the end of the school year, 16-year-old Ilsa had experienced daily panic attacks when she left her house. It took a great deal of willpower to bring herself to the doctor's office. She knew she could not return to class in the fall if her problem persisted, and she was determined not to let this happen. By using a combination of medication, coping self-talk, and gradual exposure to situations she avoided, she not only was able to return to school but even began taking driving lessons.

2. *Blocking the most distressing physical symptoms of anxiety.* Children who experience daily headaches or daily panic attacks from anxiety are suffering just as much as children who have chronic physical illnesses. Few people would argue that a child who experiences chest pains because of a congenital heart problem requires medical treatment, yet they may question the need for medication for chest pains resulting from a panic attack.

3. *Reducing a child's anxiety level in order to reduce its interference with day-to-day activities.*

> Jenny, the second child mentioned in this book, was so anxious about the possibility of vomiting in public that she couldn't get herself to eat. She was still able to leave her home sometimes to go out, but her inability to eat eventually became a medical concern. With medication she was able to begin eating, then learn coping strategies for her anxiety. Eventually, she was able to manage her anxiety without medication.

4. *Reducing the consequences of prolonged, untreated anxiety problems.* When these consequences are severe, medication can act as a "kick-start" in the process of returning an anxious child to a more adaptive way of living. Desensitization then has a better chance of succeeding.

> Mark got into angry arguments with his mother because of his fear of being separated from her. Feeling trapped by her son, Mark's mother became frustrated and angry. Her anger increased his anxiety. This further increased Mark's clinging behaviors, making his mother even more angry and generating further arguments, in a vicious circle. With a small amount of medication, Mark was able to tolerate short separations from his mother. She felt less trapped by him, so her anger diminished. As her anger diminished, Mark's anxiety decreased further and he was able to begin using coping skills to tolerate longer separations. The anger-anxiety cycle had been broken. Eventually, Mark could tolerate separations from his mother without needing medication.

5. *Treating those types of anxiety that respond particularly well to medication.* For example, children with obsessive-compulsive tendencies often respond well to medications affecting the chemical *serotonin* in the brain (Clomipramine, Fluoxetine, and Fluvoxamine are some common ones). Adolescents with panic attacks often benefit from antidepressants because these block the most severe panic symptoms. Also, if another member of your family has experienced anxiety problems and responded well to a particular medication, your doctor may suggest trying this medication with your child as well.

There are some things medication cannot do:

1. *No medication is effective 100 percent of the time.* If four out of five children with a particular anxiety problem improve as a result of taking a particular medication, this medication is considered highly effective. There is no guarantee, however, that your child won't be the one out of five who fails to improve. Many medications have lower rates of effectiveness than this. Therefore, it is worth asking your child's doctor about effectiveness before agreeing to try any medication.

2. *No medication can be guaranteed not to cause side effects in your child.* Some children experience no side effects with medication, and others (often those who are anxious about medication) experience unusual symptoms that have nothing to do with the medication they are taking. Most children will experience one or two mild side effects. Ask your child's doctor which side effects are common for a given medication (usually, those that occur in 10 percent or more of children) and which side effects are rare but potentially dangerous. Call the doctor back if you observe any of the rare side effects in your child. Other unusual symptoms in your child may result from what are called placebo effects—effects occurring when people inadvertently react (physically and psychologically) to the *knowledge* that they are taking a pill, rather than to the pill itself. People don't do this on purpose, so if it happens in your child, try to be reassuring rather than getting angry.

3. *No medication can guarantee your child a future free from anxiety-related problems.* Medications are effective only during the time they are in your child's body. Once your child stops taking the medication, a return of symptoms is possible. The reasons for stopping a medication should therefore be discussed with your child's doctor just as thoroughly as the reasons for starting it.

4. *Medication cannot give an unmotivated child the motivation to face what is feared; nor can it alter the child's basic personality.*

> Fifteen-year-old Emily experienced repeated panic attacks. Because her attacks began at school, Emily had been allowed to avoid school for almost two years. In fact, she had experienced only one panic attack during that time. This attack occurred when her previous (obviously frustrated) psychiatrist tried to physically drag her back to school. Although Emily had a number of friends and an active social life, she expressed no desire to face her fear of returning to school. Instead, she expected the school to accommodate her difficulty by providing teachers for home instruction. Her parents supported this view, feeling that Emily was too fragile to tolerate a return to school. A treatment approach similar to the one that worked for Ilsa was used. Emily took her medication but refused to take even tiny steps toward the goal of returning to school. She left treatment when she turned 16, probably because her truant officer was no longer insisting on it.

Questions to Ask the Doctor

The best general advice on the use of medication in childhood anxiety is to get a clear understanding from the doctor

- Why it is being used
- What beneficial effects it is supposed to produce
- What possible side effects and risks it entails
- How to know whether or not it is working
- What the risks and benefits of your child *not* taking the medication are

If any of these issues is unclear, ask. If it is still unclear, ask again. It is worth spending an appointment or two discussing these issues initially, rather than facing unexpected or disappointing results later. There is no such thing as a dumb question when it comes to your child's health, and nobody can treat your child if you say that you disagree. When you don't ask questions, your agreement may be assumed. This often results in problems later.

19

SPECIFIC MEDICATIONS FOR ANXIETY

Two types of medications are commonly used to treat anxiety: antidepressants and benzodiazepines.

Antidepressants

Antidepressants alter the balance of various chemicals in the brain, affecting mood. They also appear to block some of the more severe physical and psychological symptoms associated with anxiety. In children, these medications have been used for depression, Obsessive-Compulsive Disorder, and all other anxiety disorders. Most of these medications have generic names ending in the suffix -*ine*.

Effectiveness

Antidepressants do not act immediately. They take an average of two to six weeks to reach their full effect. Thus, you can't be certain whether or not the medication is working until the child has been taking it continuously for several weeks. The body does not become used to antidepressants, so these drugs can be used effectively for months or even years.

Your doctor usually estimates the dose of these medications according to your child's weight and age. As children grow and develop, they may need increased amounts of medication. The starting dose will often be low, because fewer side effects tend to be experienced when one starts low and gradually builds up to the recommended dose. Most medications cause less discomfort when starting and stopping them are done gradually. In some cases, a blood test can be done to check that the dose is the right one for your child and that the medication is not causing harm to any of the body's organs.

Side Effects

Side effects vary according to the type of antidepressant. Some children experience no side effects, whereas others experience many. Older antidepressants termed *tricyclic antidepressants* can cause dry mouth, constipation, and tiredness. Sometimes they can also affect the rhythm of the heart, a dangerous but rare side effect, so children taking them need periodic electrocardiograms. For these reasons, they are used less frequently now than in the past. Clomipramine is a tricyclic medication that is still often used, however, as it can be particularly effective for Obsessive-Compulsive Disorder.

Fluoxetine, Fluvoxamine, and other antidepressants that act specifically on the brain chemical serotonin (called selective serotonin reuptake inhibitors, or S.S.R.I.s) are used most commonly. Nausea, headaches, restlessness, and sleep problems are their common side effects. Taking these medications at a specific time of day (in the morning for the more energizing ones, in the evening for the more sedating ones) tends to reduce sleep problems. The nausea and headaches are most common early in treatment and tend to decrease with time. The use of these medications in children is relatively recent, but several studies have now shown them to be effective for anxious children. The largest study to date used Fluvoxamine, but there is no strong evidence that any serotonin-specific medication is superior to the others.

Recently, concerns have been raised about the potential for these medications to increase thoughts of suicide in some people. Most of the time, this has been reported in people with depression (rather than anxiety), and it occurs infrequently (less than 5 percent of the time, even in depressed people), but it is still a valid concern. For this reason, it is important that your child sees the doctor regularly when taking these medications, especially in the first few weeks when the risk is highest. A large recent review of studies of these medications in children concluded that the benefits of medication still outweigh the risks for most children with anxiety disorders.*

Benzodiazepines

Benzodiazepines act on the inhibitory systems in the brain. Both physical and psychological tensions decrease while the drug is in the body. These medications are used to treat anxiety, to induce sleep, and to cause muscle relaxation. Their effect lasts only as long as the drug is in the body. You can recognize these drugs by their generic names, which all end in the suffix -pam.

Effectiveness

Benzodiazepines can be used either regularly (that is, one or more times per day) or on a "p.r.n." (as needed) basis. Because the body eventually gets used to these medications, resulting in a need for increased doses, we usually use them on an as-needed basis. For example, a child who has avoided school for some time may take a benzodiazepine to get through the first period of school upon returning there. Once used to the school environment, the child can get through the rest of the day without medication. Another use is to reduce anxiety during the time when an antidepressant medication has been started but is not yet effective. In this case, the benzodiazepine is a "stop-gap" medication that allows the child to function well while waiting for the antidepressant to take effect. One very useful approach is for the older child to carry a small amount of medication (one or two tablets) in the pocket at all times "just in case" the child is overwhelmed by anxiety.

*J.A. Bridge, S. Iyengar, C.B. Salary, R.P. Barbe, B. Birmaher, H.A. Pineus, L. Ren, and D.A. Brent, "Clinical response and risk for reported suicidal ideation and suicide attempts in pediatric antidepressant treatment," *Journal of the American Medical Association*, 297: 1683–1696 (2007).

Knowing the medication is there is often reassuring to the point where it's use becomes rare. Have your child's doctor inform school or camp officials if such medication is part of your child's treatment plan. Usually, this will avoid any misunderstandings that might occur should someone see the child taking a pill in one of these settings.

Most children use these medications regularly for only short periods, because the medication eventually becomes less effective with daily use. In some instances, long-term regular use may be necessary. If your child has been using a benzodiazepine regularly for several months or longer, it should not be stopped abruptly, as this may result in increased anxiety and some physical discomfort. If your child no longer needs the medication, reduce the dose gradually under the doctor's supervision. This gives your child's body a chance to adjust.

Side Effects

The most common side effect of benzodiazepines is drowsiness. In children, this tends to be a problem only in relation to schoolwork. Reducing the dose and changing the dosing schedule so that less medication is active during the day are two approaches to this problem. It is also important to check with your child's doctor before using benzodiazepines in combination with other sedating medications (for example, antihistamines) in order to avoid extreme sedation.

Other Medications

Currently, the antidepressants and the benzodiazepines are the most common and well-studied medications used to treat anxiety disorders in children. There are other medications, however, that may also be effective, and new medications come on the market each year. Since you can't know everything about every medication, remember to ask these questions:

- Why is it being used?
- What is it supposed to do that is beneficial?
- What are the potential risks and side effects?

- How can you tell whether or not it is working?

- What are the risks and benefits of your child *not* taking the medication?

It is also worth asking about the effects of your child's medication in adults, since most psychiatric medications are not used in children until they have been proved effective for several years in adults.

Addiction

You may be concerned about your child becoming addicted to medication. Most children dislike taking medication, both because it is something adults are making them do and because it can involve unpleasant side effects. Addiction in preadolescent children is almost nonexistent. Rarely, adolescents may abuse benzodiazepines if these drugs are prescribed over a long period. Buspirone is a nonaddictive medication with effects very similar to those of benzodiazepines, and it is now being used in some anxious adolescents for this reason.

Antidepressants are not addictive, regardless of how long they are used. If addiction is a concern because of a family history of addictions or other reasons, regular monitoring by a doctor with the opportunity to ask questions and review progress is the best preventive measure.

Course of Treatment

Discuss with the doctor how long your child is likely to be taking medication. The time on medication varies from one child to the next. Usually, a child will take medication until able to return, with minimal anxiety, to all age-appropriate activities that were previously avoided. At that point, the child is encouraged to use coping skills to manage the remaining anxiety, and the medication dose is gradually decreased. Eliminating medication suddenly or during a summer holiday is not advisable, as it can result in discomfort or setbacks.

An average course of medication treatment lasts from several months to a year. Certain disorders can require long-term medication treatment. Adolescents with panic attacks, for example, may require some medication to block the attacks even after they have stopped avoiding situations. Children with severe Obsessive-Compulsive Disorder may also require long-term medication treatment.

Effects on Growth

Some parents express concern about the effect of these medications on their child's growth. Benzodiazepines and antidepressants, however, have never been associated with changes in growth. Ritalin, a drug commonly used for children with attention problems or hyperactivity, can affect growth in some cases. The only known adverse effect of long-term antidepressant use is *amotivational syndrome*. In this syndrome, children that have taken antidepressants for several years begin to appear lethargic and unmotivated. The syndrome is uncommon and resolves when medication dosage is reduced.

20

COMBINING TECHNIQUES

Several approaches to helping sensitive children cope have been introduced. These have included desensitization, an encouraging attitude, coping self-talk, relaxation, incentives, medication, and several additional strategies. Unfortunately, introducing a variety of approaches like this may leave some of you feeling that you can't see the forest for the trees. It may not be clear from what you have read so far whether your child requires one particular approach, a combination of several approaches, or none at all. It is hoped that this Key will reduce some of the confusion.

To begin, let's review the three most important facts in this book:

1. Anxiety is unrealistic fear.
2. The only way to overcome fear is to face it.
3. Anxiety is harmful to a child to the extent that it interferes with that child's ability to engage in common, age-appropriate activities at home, at school, and with peers.

Using these three facts, it is possible to examine each fear a child exhibits and decide whether or not it needs to be treated, as shown in the following decision tree.

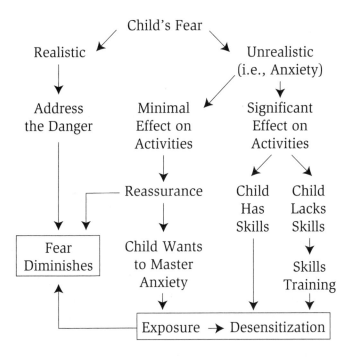

1. *First, decide whether or not the fear or some aspect of the fear could be realistic.* The following is an example of a reality-based fear.

> Mr. and Mrs. White brought their nine-year-old son, Jamie, to a therapist because of the boy's recent symptoms of separation anxiety. Jamie—a bright, outgoing boy and a promising young hockey player—had never before exhibited any symptoms of anxiety. Thorough interviews were done with Jamie, his parents, and the family as a whole. The family interview seemed strained, but no specific information came to light to explain the recent changes in Jamie's behavior.
>
> The next day, Mrs. White called to arrange an individual interview with the therapist. She admitted that she was very unhappy in her marriage and was contemplating leaving her husband. She swore she had not mentioned a word of this to Jamie, but she wondered if he might have

"picked up something" regarding her plans. The therapist agreed he probably had and suggested a frank discussion with Jamie (and her husband, of course) about her plans.

2. *When there is a real danger that what the child fears will happen, address the danger.* Telling the child to stop worrying in the face of a real threat does not make sense. Occasionally, a fear may have both a realistic component and an unrealistic component. For example, a child with a severe allergy to peanuts may check all food labels for the presence of peanuts (realistic) but also avoid the houses of all friends who report eating peanut butter (unrealistic, as going into the friends' houses will not trigger an allergic reaction unless the child eats there). In this case, only the unrealistic component should be treated as an anxiety. The child's realistic efforts to avoid peanuts should be supported.

   If you are sure a child's fear is not realistic, then it is related to anxiety (Fact 1).

3. *Anxiety that is too minor to interfere with day-to-day activities is unlikely to do the child serious harm (Fact 3).* In this case, *reassure* the child and do not pursue the matter further unless the child expresses a desire to overcome the fear. Focus on the child's strengths in other areas, and don't make a big deal about the anxiety.

4. *If there is significant interference with day-to-day activities or the child is eager to overcome the fear, then the fear must be faced (Fact 2).* Desensitization to what is feared is the cornerstone of treating anxiety. Some children will lack the necessary skills to face what is feared, especially if it has been avoided for a long time.

5. *If the child lacks the skills needed to face what is feared, some training in those skills may be needed before exposing the child to what is feared.* For example, a chronically shy child who for years has not interacted with peers may lack the social skills to do so.

Role-playing some common social situations or starting with supervised social situations that minimize the risk of the child being teased for lacking social skills may be a necessary stepping stone to putting the child into an unsupervised situation with peers (see Key 25 on shyness).

Other skills can be lost through avoidance as well. Children who are anxious about doing schoolwork independently may need to learn organizational and study skills. Children who avoid sports or games may need some practice to play these with skill and coordination. Children who avoid making any independent options may need to be prompted with multiple-choice options in order to learn this skill.

6. *Once the necessary skills have been taught, the child must learn to face what is feared through repeated exposures to it.* This is the only way to decrease your child's sensitivity. In the case of tangible fears, the feared object or situation must be faced. In the case of worries or obsessions, the dreaded thought must be stopped, faced, and challenged with coping self-talk. All other approaches described in this book so far are designed to promote exposure, which results in desensitization. Subsequent Keys describe in more detail how the various techniques can be combined to address specific anxiety-related problems.

Long-term Consequences of Anxiety

Desensitization prevents the possible long-term consequences of untreated anxiety. These consequences include a restricted lifestyle because of avoidant behaviors, a lack of coping skills, a lack of social skills, a poor sense of self-esteem, a perception of personal helplessness, and distorted family interactions around the child's anxiety. Additional treatments beyond the techniques described in this book are sometimes needed to address these long-term complications of anxiety.

Additional Treatments

Group therapy can help children whose social skills are severely impaired. Family therapy may be necessary if the anxious child is involved in destructive, circular interactions with other family members and these are interfering with the ability to cope. Individual psychotherapy may help the child learn to cope with strong feelings. Children who have experienced abuse or other serious traumas often require such therapy. A good therapeutic relationship can also enhance self-esteem.

All the treatments listed above help the anxious child most when used *in combination with*, not instead of, desensitization.

21

CHOOSING TECHNIQUES

Deciding on the best method for encouraging your child to face what is feared may require some thought. As a rule, whatever works and does no harm is best. Children vary in how they respond to the different methods of encouraging exposure to what is feared. The following list of some limitations of each approach may help you decide whether or not it is likely to work for your child:

Coping self-talk:

- Child must have some verbal ability.
- Child must be motivated to monitor own thoughts.
- More difficult in very young children.
- Works best early in an anxious episode, when child is not yet feeling overwhelmed.

Relaxation:

- Child must have some motivation to practice.
- Some anxious children are frightened by the loss-of-control sensation that may occur with deep relaxation.
- Works best early in an anxious episode, when child is not yet feeling overwhelmed.

Distraction:

- Works only early in an anxious episode; useless once anxiety has become overwhelming.

- May interfere with desensitization to feared situations.

    Reinforcements:

- Sometimes hard to find effective incentives for older children.
- Occasionally, a perfectionistic child may be so worried about failing to earn a point or sticker that anxiety worsens.

    Medication:

- Side effects.
- Children may refuse to take it.

    Encouragement:

- No problems, if done properly and expectations of child are kept realistic.

    Good health habits:

- No problems, unless you become obsessed with them.

    Other:

- No approach works 100 percent of the time.

    As shown, all these approaches have their limitations, and not all work for every child.

Giving Each Approach a Fair Trial

1. *Select the approach(es) that you think make sense for your child and apply them consistently.* Many parents feel they've tried everything and nothing worked. These parents usually devoted one or two days to each approach intermittently. Choosing an approach and following it consistently over an extended period can make all the difference.

2. *For any new approach, persevere consistently for at least three weeks.* That's how long it takes for a change in behavior to become a habit. Remember to record baseline behaviors and decide how you will measure improvement.

3. *Expect the* behavior *to change before the* feelings *do.* Many children continue to feel anxious for several weeks or even months after they have begun facing their fears and engaging in age-appropriate activities. Try to stay hopeful. Focusing on the progress that has already been made will help your child's feelings come along faster than dwelling on the remaining anxiety.

4. *If you have tried a particular approach for a reasonable length of time and no progress (not even a tiny bit) is evident, try to identify what is going wrong before abandoning your approach.* This may allow you either to modify your approach or to choose another approach where the same problem is unlikely to recur. For example:

   a) A strong-willed child has stubbornly refused to try coping self-talk even once. No progress has been made toward facing the fear. *Problem:* Coping self-talk requires motivation on the child's part, as does relaxation training. These approaches are difficult to implement with stubborn or oppositional children. *Solution:* An incentive system may be more successful, because even stubborn or oppositional children like to earn rewards.

   b) A boy with a fear of using the bathroom by himself was placed on a gradual incentive program. He was to be rewarded with a small treat for pulling his pants down as a first step. If he did not do this in five minutes, his mother would help but he would not get the treat. After one month, no progress was evident. *Problem:* Further questioning revealed that the boy did not really value treats. *Solution:* The boy loved going to school (a powerful incentive). He was told he could not go to school until he had gone to the bathroom. He quickly overcame his fear (a flooding approach).

5. *If you observe very slow progress, persist with your approach but consider adding a second one.* Continuing to model coping behavior for your child will also make a difference in the long run. Furthermore, remember that your child will continue to grow and develop in the coming years. With development, your child may be able to benefit from approaches that currently seem of little value. Just because it doesn't work today does not mean it won't work next month or next year!

PART THREE

SPECIFIC PROBLEMS

22

ANXIETY AT DIFFERENT AGES

Most children described in this book are somewhat anxious throughout their development but more seriously anxious around certain stressful times. Some of these stresses are unique to a child's experience (for example, a family separation or a move to a new house) but others reflect developmental challenges that all children encounter. Starting school, dealing with puberty, and managing the transition from elementary school to high school are common developmental challenges. Therefore, it is not surprising that more serious anxiety problems commonly surface in the early school years and soon after puberty.

The approach described in this book is ideally suited to the first group of children: those whose anxieties flare up in the early school years. Standardized treatments such as cognitive behavioral therapy have also been studied most in this age group (about age 7 to 12 years).

What if my anxious child is younger than seven years?

Younger children can still benefit from this approach, as anxious children of all ages improve when they are encouraged to face their fears. Young children may need different types of support to do this, however. For example, a young child is more dependent on her parents and may therefore be more likely to go into a feared situation when accompanied by a parent initially, whereas an older child might find this embarrassing, especially if peers are present.

Younger children also think in simpler ways than older children do. Therefore, it does not make sense to try to reassure a younger child with statements about the low probability of something frightening happening, as young children cannot understand this concept. Young children often respond better when you appeal to their imagination and provide concrete forms of reassurance. For example, have the young child imagine himself as a brave character from a favorite television show when facing a feared situation. Then, provide a reassuring object to take along (for example, a favorite small toy or a picture of the brave character) to further allay anxiety. The young child with worries may respond well to a "worry puppet" that exaggerates the fear. Have the child argue with the worry puppet and teach the puppet how to be brave. After a feared situation is faced, don't forget to provide the child with lots of praise and positive reinforcement. Most young children respond to parental praise even better than older children do. Key 13 described some further ways to talk to young anxious children.

Relaxation techniques are also helpful and fun to do with younger children. To teach relaxed breathing, have the young child lie down with a book on her stomach and make the book go up on every in-breath. Using the book ensures that breathing is deep and slow. For muscle-tensing and -relaxing exercises, young children may not have the patience to do one muscle group at a time. However, they often like metaphors such as "squeezing lemons" for clenching the arms and fists or "walking like a robot" for tensing the leg muscles. Making the arms and legs go "like a rag doll" or "like limp spaghetti" are nice metaphors for relaxing the limb muscles.

What will happen when my anxious child becomes a teenager?

At adolescence, anxiety problems tend to become less fluid. In other words, rather than having signs of anxiety come and go or shift from one area of concern to another, adolescent anxiety problems become focused on a primary area of concern. Similar to adults, adolescents may show anxiety mainly about social situations (known as social phobia), show mainly worries about future events (known as generalized anxiety), show mainly panic attacks, or some other specific set of symptoms. It is therefore helpful for parents to have separate tips for each set of symptoms. Dr. Edna Foa has written an excellent book (see resource list) about parenting anxious adolescents that contains such lists of tips for each cluster of symptoms the young person may have.

Some information applies to most anxious adolescents, however, and this will now be described. Adolescents face a number of challenges that younger children do not. Puberty can be a difficult time, especially for anxious girls who begin to outnumber anxious boys at this time. There is some evidence that this may relate to female hormone cycles, but society's expectations of teen girls may play a role as well. There is also an expectation of increasing independence at adolescence that can be particularly stressful for anxious children who are very dependent on their families (for example, children with a history of separation anxiety). Starting high school can be challenging, especially if the school is large and the teen fears getting lost or getting separated from familiar peers.

Developing one's individual identity is another key adolescent task. This task can be difficult for the child who lacks confidence and sees himself as "an anxious person" rather than "a person with an anxiety problem." When anxiety becomes part of one's emerging identity, it becomes increasingly difficult to overcome. It can also be difficult for the anxious teen who lacks confidence to assert his wishes in relation to peers. Peer pressure is difficult for all teens to resist, but it is even more difficult for anxious teens as they commonly lack assertiveness.

Some adolescents deal with their anxiety in unhealthy ways by using alcohol or nonprescription drugs. Other anxious adolescents avoid these substances entirely, fearing the detrimental effects on their bodies. Teens with social anxiety, however, are at particularly high risk of alcohol abuse. A common scenario is the extremely shy girl or boy who is offered a drink at a party and discovers that he or she is no longer socially awkward or "tongue-tied" after the alcohol takes effect. To this teen, alcohol seems like the solution to a painful, often lifelong problem. Drinking begins to increase both at parties and in other situations, until serious consequences occur.

Finally, some anxious children (the minority) begin to show signs of depression at adolescence. This occurs more often in those who have been anxious for years without successful treatment than in those whose anxiety starts at adolescence. What probably happens is that untreated anxiety and the impairment that goes with it (for example, test-taking anxiety affecting grades or social anxiety resulting in lack of friends) adversely affect self-esteem. As children with low self-esteem enter adolescence, where most people have an increased level of self-consciousness, they may focus more on their shortcomings and become depressed.

What can I do to help my anxious teen?

First, everything you did to help and encourage your anxious child will give that child a good foundation for the teen years. Children who have had even a few experiences of facing their fears are more likely to risk facing them again as they get older. Children who have learned that their parents will listen to their concerns, encourage them, and have faith in them even when they don't have faith in themselves are likely to continue to consult their parents at least some of the time when facing anxiety as adolescents.

Second, you can go back to basic principles of empathic encouragement to face feared situations and positive reinforcement for doing so. The nature of the positive reinforcement changes, of course. Teens don't typically respond to stickers or gold stars. A teen may instead value extra computer time or a chance to shop for a favorite clothing accessory. Consistent with their need for autonomy, teens also respond better when they feel they are choosing to work on a particular situation, rather than being told to do so by a parent. If the teen is motivated to work on something, ask how you can help. If the teen is not motivated, ask which situation she would like to start with and offer a couple of examples that you have already seen her do occasionally. For example, a socially anxious teen could elect to phone a friend, answer a call from a friend, or instant message a friend if that is less threatening than speaking on the telephone. Notice that you still imply that the teen will work on something, but give her a choice as to which specific thing. Also, find out activities that peers are doing (and that you approve of) that your teen may want to join, as these are often highly motivating. If your teen is not motivated to try anything, it may be worth consulting a mental health professional as some teens respond better to encouragement from people outside the family.

Third, look for ways to help your teen brush up on coping skills. Some teens like yoga or martial arts, for example, which are great ways to promote physical relaxation. Some teens can also benefit more from cognitive behavioral therapy than younger children. This occurs because teens develop the ability to think in abstract, hypothetical ways (termed "formal operations" by the developmental psychologist Piaget) that allow them to challenge their own anxious thinking more readily than younger children can.

Fourth, be alert to the problems mentioned above that may relate to anxiety. If your teen is unassertive and has friends "from the wrong side of the tracks," there is a risk of drug use or other antisocial activity. If she is socially anxious, alcohol will be very tempting for her. If your anxious teen withdraws from usual activities and appears unhappy or irritable, consider the possibility of depression. Teens do not always say they are sad or depressed, so any prolonged mood change (two weeks or more) is concerning and deserves an assessment by a mental health professional. Parenting depressed teens can be particularly challenging, so I have done a separate book on this subject (*Helping Your Teenager Beat Depression*, see resource list).

Finally, anticipate that change will always be challenging for your anxious teen, but not necessarily disastrous especially if you break it down into several steps. For example, the transition to high school can often be anticipated by breaking it down into traveling to school and navigating around the building, getting to know the teachers, organizing the workload, and making and maintaining friendships. You can then help your child problem-solve about each of these. Many schools will allow for one or more visits before the first school day in September, and some have helpful information about their staff and courses online. Teaming up with one or more friends from the previous school (assuming your child has at least one going to the same high school) can often ease the social transition.

Also allow for the possibility that your teen may have hidden strengths. For example, sometimes the desire for autonomy can be unexpectedly helpful to anxious teens. I recently saw an adolescent boy with separation anxiety that had interfered with school attendance for years, but (with support) he was able to get a summer job. He could only get to his job on the subway. Despite severe anxiety, he used the subway and soon ventured away from home and family more regularly. His confidence and school attendance improved dramatically. Thus, even though adolescence poses challenges to the anxious teen, it also brings new opportunities for psychological growth.

23

THE CLINGY CHILD

Sensitive children can respond with extreme fear to events most other children find only mildly stressful. Probably the most common example is the stress experienced by children when they are separated from their parents. Such separations, especially if sudden or unexpected, are stressful for all young children, but most adapt provided the separation is not too long and another caring adult is available. Some children, however, lack this ability to adapt to the stress of separation. They experience the separation as though it were a traumatic event and afterward anxiously cling to their parents, fearing further separations.

Eventually, these children may show a persistent fear of being separated from their parents. They may worry constantly about such separations, fear their parents will be harmed or killed if they are out of sight, or have nightmares involving themes of separation. They may have difficulty going to school alone, sleeping alone, or being alone in any setting without a parent. Like all worriers, they may complain of physical problems such as headaches or stomach pains when anticipating the event they fear (for example, being separated from their parents). A few go on to develop panic attacks in adolescence. If extreme, this problem is called *Separation Anxiety Disorder.*

In young children, some anxiety about being separated from their parents is normal. Many children shed some tears the first time they go to school or to day care. However, the child who reacts to this stress in the more extreme and persistent way described above may need help coping.

How to Help

As with any fear, the way to help is by getting your child to face it. Some parents feel uncomfortable encouraging their child to cope without them. After all, when faced with a crying, clingy child, one's first impulse is usually to provide a hug and some reassurance. In infants, this makes sense, as it promotes a feeling of security. The infant is reassured that there will always be at least one special person (the parent) who can be counted on to help if she is upset. It is thought that gradually, most infants use the mental image of their "special person" to reassure themselves when they are alone.

Some children, however, have a more difficult time forming such a mental image and consequently remain very dependent on their parents. Reassuring these children only supports their dependence and prevents them from learning how to reassure themselves. They are in the *habit* of depending on you. To help them develop alternative ways of coping, you must try to gradually change that habit.

To face the fear of separation, your child must cope with situations increasingly independently. Most parents find that a combination of gradual desensitization and incentives allows them to help their child do this. Depending on the child's age and intellectual ability, relaxation techniques and coping self-talk may also be used in preparation for going into situations independently.

Seven-year-old Annie had difficulty separating from her mother in a number of situations. She got up as soon as she heard her mother's footsteps in the morning, wouldn't go to bed until her mother went to bed, and even followed her mother to the bathroom. When her mother went to the store without her, she cried until her mother got back. Staying with a sitter was out of the question. Annie's separation behaviors were ordered according to which ones occurred sometimes, frequently, or always. Her incentive system began with the "sometimes" behaviors (crying when her mother went to the bathroom and following her mother as soon as she got out of bed). Not doing these was reinforced consistently with stars in order to work toward a small prize (one for every five stars). When Annie had mastered "sometimes" behaviors, her parents began reinforcing her for not doing behaviors in the "frequently" category. Eventually, even the most difficult challenge—staying with a sitter while her parents went out—was mastered.

Another variation on gradual desensitization is using a *transitional object*. Instead of facing a feared situation alone immediately after facing it with a parent, the child is given an intermediate step. This step consists of providing the child with a *symbol* of the parent when entering the feared situation. Most transitional objects are soft and comforting and remind the child of the parent, creating a feeling of safety. They may also promote the development of a mental image of the parent, needed for self-reassurance. Linus's blanket is a transitional object. A teddy bear, a rabbit's foot, a favorite doll, or a picture of the parent can serve the same purpose. The best transitional objects are those selected by the child.

Parents of older children sometimes wonder if a transitional object is an inappropriate crutch. It's true that transitional objects are psychological crutches, but crutches can be very useful. Using crutches after a bad ankle injury can help you get to where you must go until the ankle heals. The same is true for psychological crutches. They allow anxious children to return quickly to normal functioning while they continue to work on their fears.

Sleeping Alone

Sleeping alone is often easier if the child can take a transitional object to bed and if you create intermediate steps between sleeping in the parental bed and sleeping in a separate room. Examples are providing incentives for decreasing the number of visits to the parental bed, for gradually moving the parental and child beds farther apart, and for less frequently calling out for parental reassurance. Expect some difficult nights and try to ignore these, focusing on the better ones instead.

If going to sleep is a problem, focus less on sleep and more on quiet coping. Sleep is not entirely within children's control, but remaining in their rooms quietly certainly is. Provide incentives for gradually taking up less parental time in the evenings before settling in bed (perhaps a point for every five minutes less than the baseline), regardless of when sleep actually occurs. Award points the next morning though, as arguing about them in the evening can further interfere with sleep.

Another interesting observation I have made over the years is this: Independent sleep happens when parents decide it must happen, not before. Children of almost any age will still seek parental comfort at night as long as they are allowed to do so. It is an anxious habit that is rarely outgrown, but almost always settles down when parents make a firm decision that it must change and support each other's efforts to change it.

24

SCHOOL REFUSAL AND PANIC

School refusal can be a particularly difficult behavior to change. It is often related to separation anxiety but can also result from unpleasant events at school that cause the child to fear it (termed *School Phobia*). Regardless of the reason, the child must face what he fears by going back. Parents can try to rectify any unusually upsetting conditions at the school (for example, talking to the principal about a bully who is tormenting the child), but the child must still go back. It may be helpful to show this Key to your child's teacher if school avoidance is a problem.

Helping with Short Absences

After a short period of absence, a flooding approach may work. The child is simply returned to school and expected to stay there, with lots of praise at the end of the day for being brave.

People at school can help by not commenting about the absence, calmly engaging the child in usual school activities (which provide distraction from the anxiety), and allowing the child to have a comforting object from home if this helps. If the child still becomes distressed, it is helpful to have a quiet spot where she can sit for a few minutes to calm down and then return her to class. If someone can encourage her to do some slow breathing, this may also be helpful. Calling the parent to remove the child from the school is usually not helpful, as it reinforces the distressed behavior. Some children with separation anxiety are reassured by calling their parents' cell phones, but this easily becomes a habit so should only be allowed as a temporary stepping stone to managing school independently, with positive reinforcement for decreasing the frequency of calls.

Helping with Longer Absences
Longer absences are far more difficult to treat. Because school attendance is compulsory and education is highly valued in our society, tempers often flare around this problem, leaving parents feeling blamed and frustrated as they struggle unsuccessfully to get the child out the door each morning. When school avoidance becomes entrenched, no reward in the world may be sufficient to motivate the child.

1. For longer absences, combine the *incentive* for facing the feared situation with a *disincentive* for not facing it. For the school-refusing child, the disincentive may be sitting in a barren room until the end of the school day with no toys, telephone, or amusements whenever he does not go to school. Losing all television privileges can be another powerful disincentive. The intention is not to punish the child but rather to improve the odds that the child will choose to face the feared situation. Also, remember that all such disincentives work best when administered in a calm, neutral tone of voice.

2. *Avoid home tutoring.* A child who is tutored at home has little reason to return to school. After all, school absence is no longer affecting his grades, and the child has been relieved of the anxiety of facing what is feared (that is, school). The use of tutors in the school building may offer a nice stepping-stone to returning to class, especially for children who are very anxious about large classroom situations. Don't expect the school to provide them, though. It is up to you to negotiate a plan with the school that is feasible and meets your child's needs.

3. Identify and address any *factors at school* that are contributing to the anxiety (for example, bullying or undue criticism by a teacher).

4. Identify *school activities* the child takes pride in or that provide a sense of connection with the school. Focusing on these activities may enhance the child's motivation to return to school.

5. Identify *people who work most effectively* with the child. Sometimes one parent has less difficulty than the other getting the child to school. If so, that parent should escort the child consistently until regular attendance is reestablished. In other cases, a peer or an adult outside the family is more successful in this role. This does not mean that the parents are doing something wrong in relation to the child, as most children respond better to some people than others when it comes to school attendance.

Expect setbacks after weekends and holidays. When a child doesn't have to face what is feared for an extended period of time, the positive effects of desensitization are gradually lost. For this reason, school-refusing children often find Mondays worse than other days of the week. For holidays, especially the long summer break, it may be helpful to involve your child in activities occurring in or around the school building to ameliorate this effect.

Panic Attacks

The adolescent who has panic attacks at school may require additional help. Panic attacks are sudden, intense episodes of anxiety that appear to come "out of the blue" with no obvious trigger. Symptoms can include palpitations, sweating, trembling, shortness of breath, the feeling of choking, chest pain, nausea, dizziness, numbness or tingling, chills or hot flashes, feelings of unreality, the fear of going crazy, and the fear of dying. These symptoms are thought to occur when adrenaline (the fight-or-flight hormone) is suddenly released in the body. They almost never occur in young children but become increasingly common in adolescents and young adults. If they occur frequently or are very disabling, the condition is called *Panic Disorder*.

Adolescents with this problem will often avoid situations where they have previously experienced panic attacks, or similar situations. Those who experience an attack at school may, understandably, be reluctant to continue going there. Some can cope by working on relaxation techniques and coping self-talk to "ride through" their attacks. It is helpful for adolescents to remind themselves that

1. Once it starts, it is usually impossible to stop an attack so don't try to fight it.
2. In most people, an attack will subside on its ownwithin about half an hour (as the body runs out of adrenaline).
3. Panic attacks are never fatal.
4. The worst that can happen is for the sufferer to hyperventilate to the point of fainting momentarily, but even this is rare. Sit or lie down if you feel lightheaded.
5. Just because you have one attack doesn't mean panic attacks will happen for the rest of your life. Only a small proportion of people who experience one attack go on to have them frequently.
6. Leaving the situation in which the attack occurs doesn't help and increases the chances of avoiding that situation in the future. It is better to just wait for the attack to pass.
7. Panic attacks are disabling only if you let them stop you from doing things.
8. Panic attacks are physiological. They are not a sign of weakness.

Adolescents who experience frequent panic attacks often respond well to antidepressant medications. These medications usually decrease the intensity of the attacks and may eliminate them completely; however, they will *not* motivate the adolescent to return to school or other avoided situations—only facing these situations will cure the avoidance. Even if you are opposed to medications, it is worth consulting a physician at least once, since certain medical conditions (for example, thyroid problems) can produce panic attacks even in people with no previous history of being anxious.

25

SHYNESS AND SILENCE

Shy children show a persistent fear of social situations or situations where they risk embarrassment (for example, talking in front of the class). They are unusually self-conscious and often quite critical of themselves. Their thoughts constantly revolve around the (usually harsh) judgments they believe others are making about them. Because of this sense of inadequacy and fear of being judged, they are reluctant to approach other children. Some protest when adults try to force them into social situations; therefore, other children may mistakenly assume that they are unfriendly or odd in some way. In fact, these children usually respond very well to friendly approaches by other children. They want to relate to people but are terribly afraid of embarrassment.

Consequently, shy children tend to avoid social situations to the point where avoidance interferes with normal activities such as making friends or playing in the school yard. The longer social situations are avoided, the less opportunity these children have to develop social skills. Eventually, they do behave oddly in comparison with their peers because of this lack of social skills. Their interactions with others become less successful, and their worst fears about embarrassment are realized. Further avoidance occurs as a result, creating a vicious circle. If extreme, this condition is called *Social Phobia*.

Mark was a shy eight year old who spoke very little to other children and not at all to unfamiliar adults. He blushed and became embarrassed when asked questions in class. He avoided eye contact. He tended to slouch and stand away from other children to avoid being noticed. Mark did well at school but was often called names because of his avoidance of sports and other group activities. He had only one friend, who was also considered odd by the other children. A teacher once tried to force Mark into a game with others at recess, but as he had never played before and didn't know the rules, Mark was soon teased and relegated to the sidelines. He avoided other children even more after that day.

As his contact with people at school diminished, Mark became more preoccupied with his family. Because they were his only source of comfort, he started worrying about losing them. He became increasingly clingy with his mother. She got frustrated and angry at Mark for being so dependent, as his dependency increasingly interfered with her life. Feeling rejected at home and at school, Mark started considering himself "weird."

How to Help

The best way to help children overcome shyness is to help them face the social situations they fear. Unfortunately, there's a catch: It is very difficult to cope with social situations when you have no idea how to behave there. Mark's teacher tried to help, but the attempt backfired.

Social Skills

Shy children often lack the social skills necessary to handle social situations competently. To overcome this deficit, they may have to be taught some skills (for example, learning the rules of common games) and they may have to approach social situations in a gradual fashion. Pushing the child into a group of other children is often overwhelming. Start with what the child is already able to do. Mark's relationship with one other child suggests that he already has some ability to relate to others one to one. Pairing him up with another child (perhaps one who is more outgoing than his "odd" friend) may be a better first step than exposing him to a group. Once Mark can relate to a variety of children one to one, it may be more reasonable to get him to relate to two or three at a time.

Children who find even this approach too threatening may have to role-play common social situations with an adult before attempting to approach peers. Allow the child to play the "expert" or the more confident child, while you play the meeker one. Giving your child a chance to play teacher is often a good confidence booster.

Practicing

Having developed some basic social skills, your child should now be encouraged to start practicing them. As described for Mark, do this in a gradual, stepwise fashion. Reinforcing progress with praise or incentives may increase motivation.

1. Encourage your child to *invite* any new friends over to your home, or allow the child to go to theirs. This increases the chance that school-yard acquaintances will eventually become close friends.
2. *Model* social interactions with others in your home. If you don't value and nurture friendships, it is unlikely your child will learn to do this.
3. Once your child can relate to several children without too much discomfort, encourage participation in at least one *after-school activity.* A team sport or organized children's club (for example, Cub Scouts or Brownies) is usually most conducive to further social interactions, but make sure the child has a genuine interest in the activity. Drama clubs are excellent, as they provide plenty of opportunity for your child to overcome embarrassment. Also, it is often easier to relate to others when your child is "just pretending," as this reduces self-consciousness.

If your child repeatedly gives up on such activities after a few sessions, make a contract. Agree to a fixed number of sessions (usually, something between five and ten) that the child is expected to attend. If at the end of the contract, the child still doesn't enjoy the activity, it is probably because of a lack of interest rather than anxiety. This approach also reduces your frustration with repeatedly paying large amounts of money for sessions the child refuses to attend.

Teachers can often help by identifying a potential "buddy" to help the shy child begin socializing. The ideal buddy should be well-liked by peers (to expand social contact) but not too aggressive (as this may frighten the anxious child). Giving the shy child a special role in a group activity can also help, as most people are less self-conscious (and therefore less easily embarrassed) when they have a job to do. Teachers can help further by encouraging the shy child to volunteer answers to questions in class, but not putting him on the spot. Quietly keeping a tally of questions answered without displaying this to peers is often helpful. At the end of the week, the child can be positively reinforced for the answers offered (regardless of accuracy), or the parents can be informed so they can provide a reward at home. Shy children are also exquisitely sensitive to teachers who raise their voices, often assuming that any angry or critical comment is directed toward them personally. Help your child challenge this assumption, but also encourage teachers to set limits calmly when managing classroom behavior.

Selective Mutism

Like Mark, some (but not all) shy children also have difficulty speaking outside the home. This condition is called *Selective Mutism*. It is selective because the child refuses to speak only in certain situations. Usually, the child is quite verbal within the immediate family. In some cases, the child has a past history of speech or language difficulties (for example, stuttering) or has learned English as a second language. These factors create an embarrassment about speaking that becomes habitual. For other children, their mutism is simply an extension of shy behavior.

How to Help

All the recommendations for shyness also apply to selectively mute children. However, these children may proceed at a slower pace than shy children who speak. They may also fall behind academically, because they do not participate in class.

Most parents of these children must *work out a program with their child's school to gradually increase speech.* Again, the focus is on providing incentives for gradually increased speech. Some schools are able to help the child speak one to one with an adult (for example, a special education teacher) or participate in a small group for at least part of the day. The child can use these opportunities as stepping-stones to participation in the larger class. Also, the child's regular teacher can help by asking the child questions with multiple-choice or one-word answers. "What is the capital of Virginia?" tends to be easier than "Why did the character in this story behave as she did?" because it can be answered in a single word. Any attempt at speech is positively reinforced. If the child is embarrassed about receiving special attention at school, signs of progress can be quietly recorded by the teacher, who then informs the parents so that the effort can be praised and rewarded at home.

Building on the child's ability to speak at home can also help. Bringing friends or teachers from school into the home may allow the child to begin speaking to them in familiar surroundings. Conversely, having a parent in the school for part of the day may make it easier for the child to speak there. Both maneuvers are designed to bridge the gap between situations where the child can already speak and situations where the child cannot.

Children with Selective Mutism that has gone on for several months often benefit from S.S.R.I.s to reduce their anxiety (see Key 19), in combination with all of the other interventions already mentioned to encourage speech.

More information about helping your child overcome Selective Mutism can be found in the book *Helping Your Child with Selective Mutism* (see resource list).

26

UNASSERTIVENESS

Sensitive children often have particular difficulty asserting themselves appropriately. Without such assertiveness, they may appear meek and be vulnerable to bullies outside the home. Parents may not notice the problem at home, where the child feels safe and therefore can appear assertive or even bossy. Alternatively, the anxious child may remain unassertive 95 percent of the time by suppressing angry feelings and have occasional explosions of rage when such feelings are discharged. This style is often observed in anxious boys, who accordingly are sometimes incorrectly labeled as having behavioral disorders.

As they become better able to handle their anxieties, many children feel an increased sense of self-esteem. This allows some to begin demonstrating a more confident, assertive interpersonal style on their own. Other children, however, may need more specific help with assertiveness.

How to Help

1. It can be helpful to *role-play* with these children situations where they must say clearly what they want or poliely say "no." Often, they can learn to use techniques similar to those used by assertive adults. Again, let the child play the expert, if possible.

2. Allowing the child to make *minor decisions*, asking for the child's preferences on day-to-day matters at home, and indicating that you value the child's opinion

(although you as the parent still have the final say on major decisions) will also encourage an assertive style.

3. Clearly, it is very helpful if you can also *model* assertive behavior for your child.

Dealing with Teasing

Being assertive can be particularly difficult when a sensitive child is teased. The child may become physically aggressive but usually lacks the ability to fight with words. Furthermore, shy children's lack of eye contact and submissive posture make them obvious victims in the eyes of a bully.

1. Encourage your child to *look proud*, even if at first it's an act. People become assertive by behaving assertively. If you can stand tall and look people in the eye, you're more likely to attract the kind of attention you want and less likely to attract a bully.

2. Remind the child that if people tease, it's usually *their problem*. Teasers are trying to make themselves feel better by putting down others. They have a problem with being insecure. Discuss this with your child repeatedly, whenever teasing occurs. Also, rarely is there a school where all the other kids tease your child all of the time. Encourage the child to remember those children who have never or only rarely shown hostility, and to start approaching them more.

3. When teasing does occur, help the child come up with some simple *verbal responses*. Chances are, the child may already have overheard some common ones (for example, the old saying "Sticks and stones may break my bones but names will never hurt me" or "That's what you think!"). Praise the child for dealing with teasing situations without reacting emotionally. Crying or lashing out in anger just makes your child appear foolish, and this encourages the person teasing your child to continue.

4. If your child has one or more friends at school, encourage *proximity to those friends* at recess. There is strength in numbers, and isolated children are more likely to be victimized than children in a group.

"Just ignore it" is usually not good advice. Some children can train themselves to silently walk away from teasing, but it's hard to do so. That behavior also fails to address the emotional hurt the child feels when the teaser's comments are taken to heart (which it commonly is in shy children). Help the child use coping self-talk as well as making assertive statements to the teaser. Most teasers' comments are either not true or grossly exaggerated. Help your child evaluate whether or not there is any truth to the criticism, as well as remembering that the person teasing has a problem with insecurity.

Telling the teacher is an alternative solution but often gets your child labeled a crybaby. It is better if the child learns to handle peer situations without adult intervention, because adults can't provide protection all the time. There is one exception: When your child is in a physically dangerous situation, an adult must become involved—no child should have to endure violence at school. If your child fears being labeled a tattletale when approaching a teacher in this case, tell her that tattling is designed to get someone *into* trouble, but reporting bullying gets someone *out of* trouble. Also, ask if the school has considered an anti-bullying program, as other children besides yours may be at risk.

27
OBSESSIONS AND RITUALS

Some children are bothered by recurrent intrusive thoughts or images that disturb them. As a result, they may feel compelled to do certain activities repeatedly, even though the activities don't make a lot of sense. The process is similar to the children's game "Step on a crack, break your mother's back." The intrusive thought (obsession) is of harming one's mother. The ritual (or compulsive behavior) is to religiously avoid stepping on all sidewalk cracks in order to protect Mother. Children who exhibit this behavior to the extreme, however, may spend hours each day on their obsessions and compulsions, to the point where normal activities are neglected. This condition is called *Obsessive-Compulsive Disorder*, or OCD.

Seven-year-old Cathy did very well at school. She got into trouble, though, when her teacher refused to show her where she made her one (and only) mistake on a math test. Cathy felt this was so incredibly unfair that she threatened to throw a pencil at her teacher and was promptly sent to the office. Another day, Cathy's brother made it home from school before she did. This, too, "wasn't right" in Cathy's eyes. After all, she was older and should therefore get home first. She was so angry that she thought she could have killed him, but instead she went to her room. Frightened, she started praying "in case something deadly happens to him." Eventually, this became a habit whenever her brother upset her, and she figured out a way to protect him even better: She said the same prayer exactly 16 times. Because 2 times 2 is 4, and 4 times 4 is 16, Cathy was sure 16 was the "perfect" number.

Many anxious children show Cathy's rigid thinking about rules and fairness. As described earlier, insisting that other people do things "just so" probably represents a desire to control one's fears by making the environment more predictable.

What is different about Cathy is (a) the intensity of the anger she experiences when people don't do as she thinks they should, and (b) her unusual way of dealing with angry feelings. Instead of yelling at her brother, she internalizes her anger and converts it into the fear that something awful will happen to him. It is as though her thoughts about killing him could actually kill him. Furthermore, she attributes an almost magical significance to the number 16, resulting in the repetitive prayer. It is as though this action could undo the harm she has wished upon her brother.

A difficulty with strong emotions (particularly anger and sexual feelings), the inability to clearly distinguish harmful thoughts from harmful behavior, and a belief that the harmful thought can be undone by some form of repetitive ritual all characterize children with true obsessions and compulsions. The irrationality of these ideas and the time consumed by the rituals show that these children are clearly less well adapted than their milder counterparts who just display rigid thinking.

Cathy's praying/counting ritual was deliberately described to dispel a common misconception. People often think that if their child is not unusually neat or unusually clean, the child cannot have obsessions. This is simply not true. Some children with this problem do repetitively wash their hands, but others count repeatedly, check things repeatedly, touch things repeatedly, and so on. Some realize their behavior is irrational and will say apologetically, "My mind made me do it," but others believe more strongly in the protective effect of their rituals.

It is also important to realize that obsessions are not the same as worries. Worried children may spend long periods of time thinking about potentially dangerous or embarrassing situations (for example, failing a test) and trying to mentally prepare themselves. Unlike obsessions, however, worries can actually come true. There is usually a possibility (albeit a small one) that the situation will happen. Obsessions, by contrast, contain magical or unrealistic thinking. For example, it is very unlikely that Cathy's brother will actually die if she fails to pray.

How to Help

Some children, when they are stressed, display transient rituals for a few days or a couple of weeks. Alleviating the stress and temporarily providing some extra emotional support is helpful for these children.

Those children whose rituals persist for longer periods, however, usually require professional help. The principles used to help these children are no different from those used to help other sensitive or anxious children, but obsessions and compulsions tend to be more difficult to change than many other anxiety-related problems. Below is a description of some of the behavioral techniques a therapist may use. Familiarity with those techniques the therapist is using may allow you to help your child practice them at home. Thus, you may be able to help your child progress more quickly. Combining these techniques with medications, particularly those that act on the brain chemical serotonin (described in Key 19), is often more helpful than using either treatment alone.

To help your child overcome obsessions, the obsession must be confronted so its validity can be challenged using coping self-talk. Unfortunately, once your child is engaged in a ritual, the anxiety produced by the initial obsession (in Cathy's case "something awful will happen to my brother" or "I will cause harm to my brother") is decreased, so there is little motivation to confront the obsession.

Stopping Rituals

1. To deal with this dilemma, most therapists get the child to stop the rituals first (termed *response prevention*). Rituals are a maladaptive way of reducing anxiety. Stopping the ritual will increase anxiety (in the same way that going into a feared situation increases anxiety), resulting in desensitization. For example, Cathy must stop praying 16 times when she feels the urge to do so. Prayers once at bedtime may be appropriate, depending on one's beliefs, but 16 times is clearly excessive. Similarly, a child who exhibits compulsive hand-washing in response to obsessive fears about dirt or germs can face the fear by washing only when it's appropriate (for example, before meals) and not washing when she feels the urge to do so.

   As with any desensitization program, your child should start with the easier situations, where the urge to do the ritual is only mild, and gradually move toward the more difficult ones. Praise and reinforcements can be provided at times when the child is able either to not do the ritual or to at least interrupt it before finishing. Doing a relaxation exercise as an alternative to the ritual may help as well.

2. To motivate children, therapists often *label the ritual* with a name the child finds acceptable. The idea is for the child, the therapist, and the family to team up against the ritual. Thus, the behavior becomes the enemy, not the child.

3. Once the rituals stop, the child is far more likely to *talk about the upsetting thoughts* behind them. A few children are so embarrassed by the thoughts that they never discuss them, and that's OK as long as the child's rituals decrease and the child's ability to function improves. If the upsetting thoughts are discussed, children can be helped to find coping thoughts to replace them and eliminate the need for a ritual. The most important thinking change for the child is usually recognizing that horrible thoughts don't necessarily result in horrible actions. People can have all kinds of horrible thoughts, but they usually choose not to act on them.

More information about helping your child overcome OCD can be found in the book *Talking Back to OCD* (see resource list).

Stopping Obsessions

Some children have no rituals but are still plagued by obsessional thoughts. The child's mind is like a record that gets stuck: The same tune is played over and over again. Unable to think about other things, the child does tasks very slowly or not at all when this happens. Obsessions can be paralyzing and very unpleasant. For this reason, it is worth helping the child reduce them. Stopping obsessions is usually more challenging than stopping rituals, and almost always requires the help of a therapist. Some techniques helpful for adults and adolescents are described by Drs. Foa and Wilson in their book *Stop Obsessing!* (see resource list), which may be useful in combination with therapy if your child is older and suffers from obsessions.

As with any desensitization program, working on rituals and obsessions daily will produce the best results.

28

OTHER UNUSUAL HABITS

Some sensitive children have unusual habits that are not linked to any obvious obsessions or thought problems. For example, some children pull out their hair repeatedly (termed *Trichotillomania*), bite their fingernails or toenails repeatedly, or suck their lips nonstop. They usually experience a relief of stress or tension when they do this. Once the behavior becomes habitual, however, the child may lose the awareness of doing it. The less aware the child is of performing the behavior, the more difficulty the child has controlling it.

How to Help

These children often do well with the same approach described previously for rituals. First, the child is trained to recognize the behavior as it is happening and interrupt it (response prevention). Later, the child begins to recognize the tension preceding the behavior, often described as the "urge to do it," and is encouraged to find other ways of dealing with this tension. As with any desensitization program, working from "easy" situations—those where the child already has some control—up to more difficult ones is usually best. For habitual behaviors, any situation where the child is alone and bored (for example, watching television alone) is usually the most difficult to master.

Other helpful strategies include the following:

1. *Covering the affected area to limit the behavior.* For example, if the child pulls hair, the scalp is covered with a cap; if the child is a nail-biter, the fingertips are bandaged.

2. *Using incentives to gradually improve the child's control.* For example, children who pull their hair can put the letter *P* on the calendar when they catch themselves pulling and the letter *U* when they experience but resist the urge to pull. Points can be awarded for doing this, with *U*s worth more than *P*s. As control improves, the child can be rewarded for not pulling at all for certain time periods or for resisting the urge in increasingly difficult situations.

3. *Finding a more socially acceptable alternative behavior for the child.* Because hand and mouth behaviors are often a child's way of soothing distress, relaxing activities can be good substitutes. For example, one little girl who constantly bit her nails was musically inclined and learned to play her favorite piece on the piano whenever she was tense. Having a box of "fiddle things" to use at times when pulling is likely (for example, while watching television) can also help. Squeezeballs, worry beads, or other small items that busy the hands and appeal to your child can be kept in the box. Keep the box handy wherever pulling is likely to occur.

4. *Labeling the feeling (usually, "mad," "sad," or "scared" in younger children) and helping the child deal with the source of the tension.* You can do this if you know why the child might be distressed.

5. *Help the child identify when pulling is about to occur,* as some children are unaware of the process. Placing a dab of strong perfume on each wrist gives your child a quick reminder whenever her hand is moving up toward the scalp.

Children who do not respond to these simple interventions may need a thorough assessment by a mental health professional. For example, some children engage in these habits in response to ongoing tension in the family or at school. Addressing these sources of tension can help, and if the problem persists, a special type of therapy termed *habit reversal therapy* is sometimes recommended. More information about helping children with this problem can be found in the book *The Hair Pulling Habit and You* (see resource list).

Tics and Tourette's Syndrome

A few repetitive behaviors are only very minimally under the child's control. These consist of repetitive movements, called *tics*, or repetitive words the child speaks, especially swear words. Children who have several such behaviors may be suffering from a condition called *Tourette's Syndrome* and may require medication. Children who have only one or two tics often respond to the approach just outlined for rituals and other repetitive behaviors. Because repetitive movements can be caused by several diseases of the brain that are *not* related to anxiety, they should always be assessed by a physician.

There is good evidence that children who are severely disabled by obsessions, compulsions, unusual behaviors, or tics have a biological reason for their problems. They probably have abnormal levels of certain brain chemicals. Therefore, they are more likely than other sensitive children to benefit from medications.

29

PERFECTIONISM, DELAYING, AND LYING

A
lthough the behaviors discussed in this Key initially
sound very different, they all relate to one fear commonly found in sensitive children: the fear of failure.
Because of the thought distortions common to them, sensitive
children tend to underestimate their own abilities and overestimate others' expectations of them. Furthermore, they often see
success and failure as absolutes (all-or-nothing thinking),
meaning that anything less than total success is considered a
failure.

Perfectionism

Perfectionism is the belief that any mistake or flaw, no matter how minor, is unacceptable. For children to overcome this
belief, they need to be helped to see the world in less extreme
ways. For example, help your child to recognize the following:

- Partial success is OK—the effort still counts.
- Not being good at everything is OK—you probably have at
  least one area of strength you can use to cope.
- An imperfect appearance is OK—the world would be boring
  if we all looked the same. (Or, beauty is in the eye of the
  beholder.)
- Occasionally being a few minutes late is OK—what's the
  worst that can happen?

You get the idea.

Don't be too self-critical in front of your child. Your effect as a role model is quite powerful. If you tell the child, "It's OK not to get As in every subject" but cannot forgive yourself for being five minutes late for work, your child is unlikely to be reassured. Long assignments tend to be most challenging for perfectionistic children. Teachers can help by encouraging brainstorming and rough drafts to start assignments. Breaking the assignment into chunks also makes it appear more manageable, reducing the tendency to feel overwhelmed and avoid it. Some children are so paralyzed by their fear of mistakes that they need to have work completion reinforced for a while *regardless of accuracy*. Giving time extensions on assignments rarely helps, as it just increases the tendency to dwell on possible imperfections in the work.

Procrastination

Perfectionism can contribute to procrastination, or the tendency to delay activities. If you believe that every decision you make must be the right one—and perfectionists usually assume there is only one right one—and you have a terrible fear of making mistakes, you will eventually avoid decisions altogether. The more decisions a task involves, the more likely you are to avoid it. This is procrastination.

A sense of helplessness can also cause procrastination. After repeatedly perceiving themselves as unsuccessful, perfectionistic children may give up trying, believing a task is too difficult before even attempting it. This is particularly likely to occur with larger tasks such as school projects. The child says "I'll do it" to be compliant, but doesn't really believe that "it" is possible. Alternatively, the child may argue and refuse to try.

Following are ways to deal with procrastination:

1. Help the child gain some perspective on the task's difficulty in comparison to the child's abilities. It helps if the child has done similar tasks in the past.

2. Show the child that the task that appears so overwhelming can be broken down into small, simple steps. Encourage the child to try the easiest or most interesting steps first. It helps if you can find a way to make it fun. If necessary, reinforce the more difficult steps.

3. Gradually, allow the child to assume more responsibility for the process of doing tasks or projects. Reinforce doing at least some aspects of the task before asking for help, or make a contest out of it—for example, tell the child, "Let's see how many questions you can do before I get back," and follow up with lavish praise if even one question is attempted independently.

Some sensitive children use procrastination as a way of involving parents in their difficulties. Such children have developed the habit of using parental attention, even if it is negative attention, to reassure themselves. If you suspect this is the case, try not to get angry, for this worsens the child's anxiety. Instead, give the child a definite time limit, provide an incentive for doing whatever is feared, and leave the situation. It often helps to phrase this as a challenge.

Terry was very anxious about doing mathematics. Whenever he had math homework, he appealed to his mother for help, often before attempting a single question. Instead of arguing, Terry's mother decided to give him the egg-timer challenge: Terry was given ten minutes alone in his room to do as many math questions as he could. He got one point for every question attempted (as shown by penciling in at least part of the solution) and two points for every question completed, regardless of whether or not it was correct. The points could later be exchanged for cash. By collecting points, Terry could also work towards a trip to a fast-food restaurant with his mother, thus getting the positive attention he really craved. Within a few months, he described math as "no sweat."

If your child won't attempt the task despite these efforts, don't persist. Further unsuccessful attempts to convince the child will only increase your frustration and anger, which in turn will increase the child's anxiety. Sometimes it is best to let the chips fall where they may. Let the child take the natural consequences of his behavior. In the example above, were Terry not to do his homework his mother could let him deal with his teacher's reaction the next day. This would serve as an incentive to do homework in the future, as well as reassuring Terry that an altercation with a teacher is survivable (something many anxious children doubt).

Lying

Lying is a particularly upsetting behavior for many parents to deal with. Often, sensitive children are perceived as being vulnerable and sweet. Therefore, their parents feel terribly disappointed when the child does something "bad" like lying. With the exception of children who have severe conduct problems, most children lie to avoid punishment when they feel they have done something wrong. Sensitive children are no different from their peers in this regard. However, the sensitive child tends to do two things other children don't: The child overestimates the magnitude of the misbehavior (because any imperfection in behavior is considered a crime) and overestimates the magnitude of the likely punishment. Thus, even minor indiscretions cause the child a great deal of worry and may prompt lying. An angry reaction from the parent confirms the child's worst fears about punishment, and it increases the probability of further lying in the future.

Stay calm, and deal with the lie like any other behavior to be discouraged. Don't take it personally. Giving too much negative attention to the behavior will just make it worse. Find an appropriate disincentive for lying and try to administer it in an emotionally neutral tone of voice.

In addition to the specific suggestions for teachers in the last few Keys, some general teaching principles to help anxious children include:

1. Avoid undue time pressure. "Minute math" is a nightmare for most anxious children.
2. Allow the child to use memory aids or cue cards to reduce performance anxiety with presentations.
3. Praise for a job well done or for giving it a good try is always more motivating than criticism for mistakes or failure to complete an assignment.
4. Predictable classroom routines reduce anxiety. Always having the spelling test on the same day of the week and always posting due dates for projects consistently in the same place are two examples.
5. Teachers who model calm behavior tend to inspire it in their students.
6. Include some relaxation exercises for the whole class at times of stress (for example, the week before examinations). One resource specific to schools is *Taming Your Dragons: A Collection of Creative Relaxation Activities for Home and School* (see resource list).
7. When addressing specific anxieties that impact a child's school life, good communication between home and school is essential and very reassuring to the child. Many parents and teachers use e-mail for this, reducing the need for lengthy meetings and allowing same-day "course corrections" if a child is not responding well to a particular intervention.

30

WHEN THE DANGER IS REAL

Given the current level of violence in society, parents often wonder how they can help their children deal with anxiety about current events. Abductions, murders, and other forms of violence affect all our lives, and children are not exempt. If anything, they are more vulnerable than adults to becoming victims.

Furthermore, children can't avoid hearing about such events. If parents don't discuss them, children hear about them through peers, television, or other sources of information. Parents who pretend that scary things don't happen are not being honest with their children, and they miss the opportunity to discuss these events in a way that is helpful to the children.

When a disturbing event is receiving wide media coverage, try the following approach:

1. *Supervise the child's exposure to the event.* For example, if you know that coverage on Channel 10 is usually more gruesome and sensationalistic than coverage on Channel 5, opt for the less dramatic presentation.

2. *Invite the child to talk about it, but don't lecture.* Explore the child's thoughts and feelings about it before offering solutions. None of us are mind readers, and children often pick up on aspects of a story that adults might not even think about.

3. *Respond to the child's questions according to her level of understanding.* Avoid complicated or overly detailed explanations.

4. *Help the child put it in perspective.* Be honest about the fact that scary things can happen, but emphasize the rarity of such events. Let the child know that the vast majority of people never experience them. Remind the child that most news broadcasts contain only the bad news of the day, not the good news.

5. *Talk about how the child can decrease the risk of being hurt.* Take the opportunity to do some constructive street-proofing. Don't say, "There are bad people out there who can kidnap and kill you," without any discussion of what the child can do to reduce her risk. This approach merely increases the child's anxiety. Instead, teach the child how to handle situations that have the potential to become dangerous. The emphasis should be on *what the child can do*, not on instilling a sense of fear or helplessness.

6. *If the event has legal implications, encourage constructive action.* Children often feel there is nothing they can do to change what happens in the world, because they are not old enough to vote. It is sometimes helpful to show them what they can do. For example, a child can write a letter to her local legislator about a particular issue. Alternatively, the child can join with other children or adults to protest a particular injustice. Encouraging your child to act will decrease the helplessness and despair often produced in children by news of violence.

Post-traumatic Stress Disorder

Unfortunately, some children are exposed to frightening situations outside the range of normal human experience. Children who live through wars, natural disasters, or physical or sexual assaults are almost always affected psychologically by these traumatic events. Even children with a very low level of temperamental sensitivity usually show anxiety-related symptoms after such events. Often, they show a triad of symptoms including vivid and disturbing memories of the event (in dreams or flashbacks), avoidance of situations or feelings that provide reminders of the event (including "feeling numb" or blocking certain memories), and a high level of physical tension even when no danger is present. This triad is termed *Post-traumatic Stress Disorder.* Depending on the child's vulnerability and the nature of the event, it may persist for months or even years.

Milder cases (as when an otherwise outgoing child with little vulnerability to anxiety is exposed to a single frightening event) can often be addressed using the perspective-taking and desensitization techniques described in this book. Forcing a child to talk about the traumatic event (so-called *"debriefing"*) sometimes does more harm than good. Giving the child the opportunity to talk about it when she is ready, however, often helps her make sense of the event and integrate it with the rest of her life experience. Take your cues from the child, and seek professional help only if the trauma-related anxieties persist for several months.

Also, it can't be assumed that a single discussion will suffice. As children mature, additional questions and concerns about past traumatic events may arise. For example, a five-year-old boy whose leg was badly fractured in a car accident initially expressed concerns about mutilation. Seeing the orthopedic screws and rods used to hold the fractured bone in place, he wondered aloud if his leg would ever work again, "because of all the holes in it when the screws come out." Several years later, as a young teenager, he no longer doubted that his leg worked but was concerned that the surgical scars had made him unattractive to girls.

Children exposed repeatedly to serious trauma (for example, incest victims) are unlikely to recover fully without professional counseling.

PART FOUR

OTHERS' REACTIONS
TO ANXIETY

31

FAMILY INTERACTIONS AROUND ANXIETY

L iving with a sensitive child is not easy. Family interactions are often affected by a child's anxiety. This does not necessarily mean that the family caused the anxiety. It could just as easily mean that the family is different *in response to* the child's anxiety. By the time the child is brought to a doctor for treatment, this is often a chicken-and-egg question. In other words, self-perpetuating, destructive patterns of interaction are happening in the family but it is impossible to tell where they started. The problem is a vicious circle. Blame cannot be assigned to any one person.

The difficulty with vicious circles is that they leave everyone in the family feeling frustrated and angry. Being angry with the anxious child makes the anxiety worse and is often what keeps the circle going. The following, rather extreme, example illustrates many of the most difficult aspects of living with an anxious child. It also shows the diverse ways in which different family members can react to anxiety.

Eight-year-old Monica B. has developed intense separation anxiety from her mother. She clings and whines whenever Mrs. B. leaves her side and will not do schoolwork without her mother's help. The family struggles each morning to get her to go to school. She has one older sister, Kara, who is not anxious and does well at school.

Mr. B. sees himself as a very rational man. He minimizes Monica's anxiety, seeing no logical reason for it, and concludes that it is a deliberate attempt to draw attention to herself and to control her mother. He responds by ridiculing Monica's anxiety. He believes this will help Monica to realize how silly her fears are and does not consider how bad it makes Monica feel about herself. He is angry with his wife for allowing herself to be manipulated by her daughter and consequently neglecting him. His greatest fear is public embarrassment because of Monica's behavior. Although he is unaware of it, Monica's lack of success at school also adds insult to injury, as it reminds him of his own academic difficulties as a boy. He feels closer to Kara, taking pride in her accomplishments.

Mrs. B., on the other hand, considers herself a more sensitive parent than her husband. She interprets all of Monica's anxious behaviors as signs of genuine distress and responds by offering comfort and protection. Being mildly anxious herself, she dislikes interpersonal conflict and sometimes allows Monica to avoid anxiety-provoking situations rather than risking an argument. Inadvertently, she thus reinforces Monica's increasingly babyish behavior and allows Monica's confidence in her own abilities to decline. Over time, the behavior becomes more and more age-inappropriate. Mrs. B. begins to get frustrated with Monica and intermittently resists Monica's clinging. Unfortunately, her fear of conflict and her perception of Monica as vulnerable prevent her from resisting the clinging consistently. This intermittent reinforcement of Monica's clinging behavior serves to perpetuate the behavior.

By this time, Kara and Monica are constantly fighting. Kara usually provokes the fights, resenting both Monica's ability to avoid responsibility and her "special" relationship with their mother. Emulating her father, Kara refers to Monica as a crybaby.

Mrs. B. begins to feel very stressed at home. She sees her husband as unsupportive, because he disagrees with most of her parenting decisions these days. Kara's attitude echoes her father's, and the relationship between Mrs. B. and her older daughter becomes more distant.

If things continue to deteriorate, the marital conflict and the sibling conflict will escalate. The coalitions between Kara and Mr. B. and between Monica and Mrs. B. may become entrenched. As Mrs. B. feels increasingly overwhelmed, she may become depressed. Because the only person in the family who is still close to her is Monica, she may begin to use Monica as a sounding board for her troubles. A role reversal then occurs, with Monica emotionally supporting her mother rather than the other way around. The psychological boundary between mother and daughter is lost, making it almost impossible to address Monica's increasingly severe separation anxiety.

What Went Wrong in This Family?

For a family to work together successfully to solve problems, four things are required:

1. *Members of the family must be clear on what their roles are.* What rights and responsibilities does each member have? In general, parents have both more rights and more responsibilities than children do.
2. *Members of the family must be able to communicate effectively* in order to use the various roles to solve problems.
3. *Some flexibility must exist in family relationships* so that members each feel they belong to the family without feeling smothered by another family member. Flexibility also prevents persistent coalitions between some family members that leave others feeling excluded.

4. *Consistency must be present in how family members are treated* so that family members feel they can rely on each other and can work together feeling secure.

Let's examine how each of these four requirements has been disturbed in the B. family:

1. First, the family roles have changed. Monica's role was initially reduced to that of a baby and later elevated to that of her mother's confidante. Both roles are age-inappropriate. Because of Monica's (perceived) needs, Mrs. B. reduced her roles as wife to her husband and mother to Kara. If she becomes depressed, Mrs. B. may abdicate her parental role more completely, leaving Mr. B. as the sole authority figure in the family.

2. Communication has also changed in this family. Effective communication is direct, overt, and nonabusive. It is direct because the speaker addresses the person for whom the message is intended (for example, "Emily, please do the dishes"). It is overt because it means what it says: There is no hidden message. It is nonabusive because the speaker's goal is to solve a problem, not to derogate another person.

When family relationships become inflexible, people feel either too close to or too distant from particular family members.

When people feel excluded by other family members, they are hurt. They may express their hurt by derogating other family members, as Mr. B. has derogated Monica. They may also express it through indirect derogation, such as "Is anyone around here gonna clean up this mess?" (implying that whoever is within earshot is lazy or unclean).

In contrast, people in overly close relationships sometimes communicate as though they could read each other's minds. For example, as Mrs. B. starts to feel closer to Monica than to other family members, she might say things like "We prefer music to sports" about herself and Monica. She feels no need to ask Monica's opinion on the subject, because she assumes Monica agrees. People who communicate this way feel threatened by evidence of differences between themselves and the other person. It is more comfortable for them to assume the other person agrees, as they fear disagreements will jeopardize the relationship. Ironically, this inability to tolerate differences leaves the other person feeling coerced or controlled, resulting in anger and destabilizing the relationship. Regardless of its form, all distorted communication interferes with problem solving.

3. Flexibility has also been lost in this family. Rigid coalitions have developed between Mrs. B. and Monica and between Mr. B. and Kara. Each dyad feels hurt and excluded by the other two people. It seems as if this family of four people has almost split into two small families of two people each.

4. Finally, inconsistency has developed in the family. The difference in how Mr. B. and Mrs. B. handle Monica's behavior is obvious. Inconsistency has also developed in the relationship between Monica and her mother. Partly, this is because of the fluctuations in Monica's anxiety level. However, Mrs. B.'s desire to protect Monica and to avoid conflict also contributes to the inconsistency. Most anxious behavior at some point becomes so unreasonable that even the most protective parents decide to put their foot down. Doing this intermittently, however, just reinforces the behavior. The parent is then caught oscillating back and forth between giving in, which perpetuates the behavior, and angrily resisting the behavior, which makes the child more anxious.

None of these patterns are unique to families with anxious children, nor do all families with anxious children have such problems. These examples are merely meant to illustrate styles of interaction that cause trouble and that people can, often inadvertently, slide into in response to a family member's anxiety.

32

BEING CONSISTENT

R ecall the description in Key 5 of two ineffective ways of encouraging anxious children. You may have noticed that Mr. and Mrs. B. (Key 31) each illustrated one of these ineffective styles.

Mr. B. psychologically minimized Monica's vulnerability, resulting in:

1. Misreading her anxiety as attention seeking or manipulation, and
2. Trying to encourage Monica by trivializing her feelings, leaving her feeling ridiculed and unsupported.

Mrs. B., on the other hand, psychologically maximized Monica's vulnerability, resulting in:

1. Clearly seeing Monica's anxiety while ignoring her strengths, and
2. Trying to encourage her by showing empathy for her feelings but not expressing confidence in her abilities.

A Spectrum of Attitudes

These styles represent two extremes of a spectrum of attitudes parents can have toward their child's vulnerability.

Minimizers of vulnerability tend to be self-sufficient types, more at ease with logic than with feelings and sometimes distant in relationships. They have difficulty acknowledging vulnerability in themselves and others. Often good organizers, they easily set limits and take a calm, logical approach to children's problems. They may, however, misread others' feelings and have difficulty showing empathy.

Maximizers of vulnerability tend to value feelings more than logic and are often highly involved in and highly concerned with relationships. They tend to overestimate their own and others' vulnerability. Their strength lies in reading others' feelings and showing empathy. Their weakness lies in allowing feelings to cloud their judgment, resulting in inconsistency and difficulty setting limits with children.

Neither extreme is desirable. Ideally, parents use logic and feelings flexibly as appropriate to the situation. They can acknowledge their own and the child's vulnerability without overestimating or underestimating it. Consequently, they are able to set limits, be reasonably consistent, and show empathy for their child's feelings.

Most people are in between the two extremes but do *some* minimizing or *some* maximizing of the child's vulnerability. Spouses are rarely at exactly the same point on the spectrum, making it easy for conflicts to develop around an anxious child. These attitudes stem from parents' earliest experiences with their own parents. Minimization or maximization of distress can already be seen in 12 month olds when separated from their parents. Because people don't have clear memories of this early period in their lives, they are often unaware of having developed the attitudinal biases.

Dealing with Attitudinal Differences

1. Take a moment to *think about where you are on the attitude spectrum.* Where is your partner on the spectrum? Can you learn something from your partner's style? Can your partner learn something from your style? How can you use the advantages of each style to complement each other? When you encourage your child in the next few days, pay attention to your attitude. See if modifying your approach makes any difference to your child's success with facing what is feared.

2. *Develop empathy for your partner's position,* and consider how you could modify your own attitudinal bias to come closer to a middle ground. Because spouses usually differ in their position on the attitude spectrum, some compromise is required to develop a consistent approach for managing their child's anxiety.

3. Set aside a *time for communicating with your partner* about the child. Finding time to talk as a couple can be difficult in our hectic society, but it is essential if you are to work together successfully. Make sure there is at least one such time each week. Ideally, the child should not be able to overhear these discussions. Presenting a consistent, united front to the child is far more reassuring than allowing the child to witness parental disagreements. The following may be helpful:

   a. Begin by letting your partner know *what you like* about the way he or she handles the child, and vice versa. Doing this increases the likelihood that the two of you will build on your strengths as parents, rather than spending the whole session complaining and blaming.

   b. Identify disagreements and try to *rank the importance of each problem.* Few parents are perfectly consistent, but those who manage behavior effectively tend to be consistent in how they handle their child's most troubling behaviors. Decide what *must* change versus what you can live with for the time being.

   c. For each major problem, *brainstorm* with your partner to generate as many solutions as possible.

   d. Examine the *pros and cons* of each solution in turn, until you reach a consensus on which one is best. Don't agree to a solution just to keep the peace or it won't be followed consistently.

Remember, being consistent doesn't mean that both of you have to do exactly the same things with the child. One possible solution is to divide the work of child rearing according to your talents. For example, if one parent has real difficulty setting limits and the other parent can do this easily, it may be sensible to allow the more "disciplinarian" parent to handle most limit setting (although there will always be occasions when the disciplinarian parent is not around and the other parent will have to set limits). The other parent can help by consistently supporting the disciplinarian and assisting the child in other areas according to that parent's own talents.

e. Decide what each of you will do to *implement* your solution.

f. Set a regular *follow-up time* to evaluate progress and fine-tune your approach. Most people sometimes forget what they are supposed to do, so give yourselves a chance to review.

Persistence and patience (with your partner as well as with the child!) will pay off in the long run. A nice way to summarize this approach is provided by the mnemonic "PASTE": *P*ick a problem, list *a*lternatives, *s*elect an alternative, *t*ry it out, and *e*valuate the result.

If discussions with your partner are difficult, try these tips:

1. Don't interrupt until your partner has finished talking.

2. Before responding, try to paraphrase what your partner has just said to make sure you understand exactly what was meant.

3. Start every sentence about a point of disagreement with "I feel . . ." rather than "You always do. . ." Much of the anger in arguments comes from people feeling falsely accused or blamed for a problem.

Don't forget about the sensitive child's *siblings*. Sensitive children can require considerable attention. Find ways of attending to the other children so that they don't feel the need to develop a problem behavior just to be noticed.

What if I am a single parent? Does any of this information apply to my situation?

The same principles apply in single-parent households as in two-parent households. Single parents have the advantage of not needing to worry about having another adult disagree with their parenting practices (unless there is a disagreeable grandparent or other relative living with them), but they are burdened by having to do all the parenting themselves as well as often working and managing a busy household. In short, single parents have hectic lives. This can make it difficult to focus on the child's anxieties and to use the same approach to them consistently each time they occur.

Summary

The following is a summary of what is helpful for the sensitive child in the family:

1. Take the child's concerns seriously (rather than ridiculing or derogating), while expressing confidence in the child's ability to be brave and overcome anxious feelings. This is the most encouraging attitude for anxious children.

2. Set clear, age-appropriate expectations, with some modification for the child's needs. For example, if other children are participating in after-school activities, the anxious child should also be encouraged to participate but perhaps by starting one new activity at a time, rather than taking on several at once.

3. In order to encourage the child to face fears, provide choices with more positive consequences for the brave choice than for the fearful choice. Avoid arguing,

trying to convince the child, or trying to find out precisely what is making the child anxious. Most children can't tell you why they are anxious, and most are almost impossible to convince. Praise is often the most positive consequence.

4. Parents have more rights and responsibilities than children do. Keep it that way. Your job is not to make the child like you but to do what is in the child's best interest.

5. Consistency is very reassuring for anxious children. Giving the child the same messages consistently over time and making sure both parents agree on those messages are important.

6. Whenever possible, communicate directly, overtly, and without abusive or derogatory language. This is helpful to all family members, not just the anxious child.

7. Try to avoid anger. Some frustration with the child is natural, but outbursts of extreme anger intensify the child's anxiety, and derogatory comments reduce self-esteem.

8. Try to avoid overprotection. Like everyone else, anxious children learn from their own mistakes and so need the chance to make a few.

9. Try to avoid overinvolvement. Family members other than the anxious child need your time, too, and all parents need some time for themselves.

10. Let the child know that many other people struggle with anxiety, too. Anxiety is invisible, so many anxious children feel very different from others until they meet someone else who admits being anxious.

33

DEALING WITH THE COMMUNITY

Children in our society cannot behave as autonomous individuals. They are supervised by adults at almost all times, whether by a parent, a teacher, a doctor, a coach, or another member of the community. Helping your anxious child, therefore, will usually require some collaboration with other members of the community.

Telling Others About Your Child's Problem

It can be difficult to decide who should know about your child's problem. Many parents are concerned that others might label their child as psychiatrically ill. This concern produces a dilemma, however: Hiding the truth may create the impression that you are ashamed of the child, whereas being brutally honest can result in embarrassment for the child. The best approach is probably to look at each person with whom your child comes in contact and ask yourself the following questions:

1. *What facts do people need to know so that they can do their jobs in relation to my child?* Other facts are generally none of their business, unless the child chooses to reveal them. Similarly, people who don't have a job to do in relation to the child (for example, peers, strangers, or uninvolved relatives) do not need to know any details, unless the child chooses to reveal them.

2. *How should those facts be presented so that they are helpful to the other person without unduly stigmatizing my child?* Rather than labeling your child as anxious or sensitive, it may be less stigmatizing for the child and more helpful to the other person if you describe exactly your child's areas of strength and areas of difficulty. Include in your description any specific ways in which you would like others to modify their work in relation to your child. If disagreements arise, try to listen to the other person's point of view rather than immediately becoming critical or defensive. Once you understand that point of view, try to begin a constructive, problem-solving discussion, using the approach presented in Key 32 for talking to your partner.

If the child sees a psychiatrist, some parents substitute phrases such as "going to learn how to handle feelings" or "going to learn how to handle stress," whereas others simply state in a matter-of-fact way that a psychiatrist is involved. This is a matter of personal preference.

A prevalent misconception in the community is that anxious children are "manipulative" or "attention seeking." It is worth sitting down with people who express this view to clarify for them the reasons for your child's behavior. Even if you can't get the person to understand your child completely, helpful suggestions you provide about managing the child's behavior may be appreciated.

Occasionally, the other person is not receptive to these ideas and continues to insist that the child is "just manipulating" or starts to interfere with your management of the child. If this happens, you may be forced to limit that person's contact with your child. Setting such a limit can be particularly difficult in the case of grandparents or other close relatives, but remember: *You and nobody else are responsible for raising your child.* Don't be bullied into doing things that are clearly not in your child's best interest.

3. *Who is the best person to convey information about my child?* As a rule, the older and more mature the child, the more involved that child should be in the process. Adolescents often handle the entire issue of "who to tell" without parental involvement. For children of any age, it is inappropriate to tell your child's friends about the problem without the child's permission. Younger children may need more parental support in discussing their problem with others, especially if the other person is an authority figure. Let the child handle the situation as independently as possible. Provide help only if the child asks for it or very obviously requires it. Responding to the child's request (rather than leaping in to help) not only is more appreciated but also gives the child extra practice at behaving assertively and taking responsibility for the problem.

Your child's doctor can convey information about your child to others only with your written permission and is usually not paid for doing so. It is not surprising, therefore, that some doctors are less than eager to call your child's school, social worker, Scout leader, and so forth, on your behalf. Apply the same rule of thumb to yourself as to your children: Ask for help if you need it (for example, if the school authorities are not taking you seriously, because you are "just a parent"), but handle as much as you can yourself. In the process, you'll become more confident at advocating for your child.

Collaborating with Others About Your Child's Problem

Collaborating with other members of the community means ensuring that various people and organizations work hand in hand for the benefit of your child. Problems arise when one member of the community doesn't know what the other members are doing. For example, a psychiatrist working with a family may hear that a school psychologist is available and assume that this person will address any school difficulties the child encounters, whereas the school psychologist, on hearing that the child sees a psychiatrist, may assume that further involvement in the case is not required.

It is often up to parents to clarify who is doing what for the child and to ensure communication among the various people involved. The community surrounding your child can be compared to an orchestra: Your child's treatment won't progress harmoniously unless *you* are prepared to pick up the baton and conduct. When dealing with an organization (for example, your child's school), it is often helpful to have one contact person who understands your child's difficulties and can coordinate what other people in the organization do. Remember that you must sign a consent form for every pair of professionals or organizations who want to communicate about your child's case.

A common difficulty encountered is failing to clarify the role of each person involved (that is, expecting the system to look after the child). One illustration is the psychiatrist– school psychologist example above.

Dealing with Schoolteachers

The role of the schoolteacher in helping your child may also require clarification. Teachers must be informed if your child will regularly miss classes to see a doctor or other mental health professional. Once teachers are so informed, their response is often quite positive. In fact, some teachers wish more of their pupils got psychiatric treatment! Teachers can also be helpful in encouraging the child's integration into the peer group (for example, during their "yard duty"). They can be helpful observers, documenting changes in the child's behavior outside the home. In some cases, they can even work with parents by consistently reinforcing or not reinforcing behaviors the parents are trying to help the child change. Remember, however, that the teacher probably has 30 or so other children, many of whom have special needs. Expecting a teacher to take on the role of therapist is unreasonable.

Find out exactly what the teacher is able to do in relation to your child and what additional resources are available at the school. Start with what the teacher can do. Look back at Key 32's description of the attitudinal differences and communication tips in relation to your partner. The same approach can be helpful in discussions with your child's teacher, especially if he or she is initially unsympathetic to your child's difficulties. If the teacher doesn't seem to understand your child's difficulties, consider providing one or two Keys from this book to the teacher. Choose the one(s) that seem to best describe your child. Teachers rarely have time to read entire books, but they are often eager to have concise, practical information to help a given student. If discussions with the teacher are still not fruitful, find out what else the school can do. A talk with the school principal should give you a good idea of what resources are available and of how flexible the school is likely to be in meeting your child's needs. If discussions with the teacher and the principal do not produce a satisfactory result, find out what other available schools can do.

If alternatives to your child's present school are available, investigate them. Teachers have the most day-to-day contact with your child, but it is often the school principal who determines the atmosphere in which they teach. If you find a great teacher but the principal is unsympathetic to your cause, your child is unlikely to succeed at that school, and vice versa. School routines should also be examined, as these may be more or less anxiety-provoking for your child. For example, a child who has difficulty with change will do better at a school with the same timetable every day than one with variable timetables.

As noted in Key 24, requesting home tutoring for children with School Phobia is generally not helpful, because continued avoidance of school perpetuates the problem. Small-class placement or individual study time within the school building provides a better stepping-stone toward reintegration into the regular class.

34

DEALING WITH PROFESSIONALS

Much dissatisfaction with doctors and other profession- als can be prevented if you avoid a few pitfalls. This Key describes three common ones.

1. *Expecting the professional to look after the child's needs completely, without any monitoring from you.* A good example is the case of the busy doctor.

> Parents phone the doctor to cancel their child's appoint- ment. The doctor's receptionist records the cancellation. The parents now wait for the doctor's office to call back to reschedule the appointment. Nothing happens, and the child's treatment ends or is disrupted for a long time. Meanwhile, the receptionist fails to alert the doctor to the fact that the appointment has not been rescheduled. With dozens of patients to book, one appointment is easily lost in the shuffle. Even if alerted to the situation, the doctor may assume that the parents will call the next day to arrange another appointment.

The problem in this case is the assumption that "the doctor knows best" and will call back if another appointment is needed. In reality, most doctors don't track down every patient who cancels, and it is up to patients or their guardians to rebook.

2. *Failing to clarify the risks and benefits to be expected from a particular treatment.* This issue was discussed briefly in Keys 18 and 19 about medications. However, it is important to know the potential risks and benefits of *all* treatments, medical or otherwise. People who are unaware of side effects that are troublesome but not dangerous often stop treatment that could be beneficial. People who are unaware of what benefits to expect from treatment may have difficulty determining whether or not the treatment is helping. For example:

> A child with Separation Anxiety Disorder and Selective Mutism (not speaking outside the home) is treated with a medication. At the next appointment, the doctor is delighted to find the child able to carry on a fluent conversation. The parents, on the other hand, report "no improvement," because the child still has separation anxiety and they were less concerned about the mutism.

Clear goals, including a time frame for those goals, should be agreed upon at the start of treatment. Find out when you can expect to start seeing changes, how long it takes for the treatment to have its full effect, and how to tell if the treatment is not working. If your child is being seen individually, make a regular time to discuss your child's progress and other treatment issues. Most professionals are willing to take a few minutes at the beginning or end of an appointment to do this, if it has been agreed upon in advance. Many disappointments can be avoided by taking a little time at the beginning of treatment to clarify these issues.

3. *Failing to address dissatisfaction with another person's approach to your child.* This difficulty commonly occurs when parents, because of either personal anxiety or cultural expectations, feel uncomfortable questioning a professional's treatment of their child. When a parent disagrees with a treatment but says nothing,

there are two common outcomes. One is for the parent to pay lip service to the professional but not support the treatment at home, a situation usually resulting in treatment failure. The other is for the child and family to drop out of treatment and go elsewhere, hoping for a better treatment, a situation usually resulting in repeated assessments and inconsistent treatment and thus exacerbating the child's anxiety in the long run. The same difficulty may occur when parents and schoolteachers disagree; in this case, the outcome can be poor achievement by the child or a disruptive change of schools.

Confronting the dissatisfaction, on the other hand, gives the professional a chance to clarify the reasons for the treatment approach and to address your concerns. It may even allow the professional to incorporate some of your suggestions into the treatment approach. If major disagreements persist, the professional may be able to make a referral to someone else in the same field whose philosophy is closer to your own. Very little reassessment is needed in this case, for information can pass smoothly from one professional to the next. Disruption of your child's treatment is minimized. Again, your written consent is required for this transfer of information to occur.

Occasionally, you may encounter a professional with inflexible views that differ dramatically from your own. Every group of people contains some who can't concede they might be wrong. In this case, even referral to a more compatible professional may not be possible. It is then in your child's best interest that you seek out another professional quickly. Talk to other parents about professionals they have found helpful. Calling a major medical center, your local medical association, or your insurance company for additional names of doctors may also be worthwhile. Don't be discouraged if your child is placed on a waiting list for several months. This is to be expected, as children's mental health resources are scarce. Getting your child on several lists concurrently is usually the best approach. One of the professionals you contact is bound to have a cancellation sooner or later.

Needless to say, when you find particularly helpful professionals, hang onto them! Anxiety is characterized by exacerbations and remissions at various times in a child's development. Having the same people helping with your child's difficulties every time will ensure a consistent approach that allows your child to build on previous coping skills while developing new ones. It also prevents time-consuming and often unnecessary reassessments.

Recurrent Problems with Professionals

If you have gone to several different professionals with your child and run into similar problems every time you tried to work with a new one, take a moment to reflect on your approach. Something you are doing may be making it difficult for *anyone* to help. For example, being inflexible yourself or not listening to the professional's point of view may interfere with forming a working relationship. Listening but not following through on suggestions and then blaming the professional is another common obstacle to success. Professionals are human, and most will respond more positively if you treat them with courtesy, tell them as much about the problem as they need to know to be helpful to your child, share with them what you have already found to be helpful for your child, listen to what they have to say, and are honest about any misgivings you feel about their suggestions. Usually, you can then negotiate a treatment plan that both sides can follow.

Recurrent problems with professionals may also occur when different family members (especially parents) have a different understanding of what the professional has suggested or how to implement it. This common difficulty can be avoided if both parents try to attend appointments concerning the child, particularly the initial assessment appointment(s).

If the Situation Deteriorates

Some anxious children can deteriorate and become depressed while they are awaiting treatment. Others, who seek constant reassurance, can become so demanding that their parents feel trapped and unable to cope. If you get to the point of fearing for your child's safety or your own sanity, visit your local hospital emergency room.

The most important fact to bear in mind is this: Professionals are trained to do what is helpful for *most* children *most* of the time. There are always exceptions, and if you think your child is one of them, speak up! Educate the person you are dealing with about the particular needs of your child and say exactly what you want done. Only you can conduct the orchestra of people surrounding your child in a way that makes it easier for the child to get back on a healthy course of development.

35

WHAT IF YOU'RE STILL STRUGGLING?

If you have tried several techniques and nothing seems to be working, see if one of the following common obstacles to success is getting in the way:

1. *Trying each technique for too short a time.* Remember that three weeks is a minimum for changing a habitual behavior. The time may be longer if you are not being completely consistent in applying your technique or if unusual circumstances (for example, the child getting sick with the flu) interfere with your child's progress.

2. *Being inconsistent from one time to the next or from one person to another.* There may be subtle differences (for example, being stressed yourself and using a harsher tone of voice sometimes) in how you are applying your technique from day to day. Also, look for any differences in how you and your partner are applying it.

3. *Failing to recognize partial success.* Even the smallest change occurring only once needs to be recognized and reinforced. Otherwise, your child feels, "I really tried and nobody noticed," and gives up.

4. *Expressing too much negative emotion.* For all techniques, if you get upset your child gets more anxious. Also, your upset feelings focus attention on the child's undesirable behavior, which inadvertently encourages the child to continue it.

5. *Having unrealistic expectations.* Any technique can change only one specific behavior in one specific situation. Expecting the child to be able to change other behaviors that are similar to the one on which you have focused or expecting the child to apply newly found coping skills to other situations is unrealistic. Feeling disappointed because of such expectations also interferes with your ability to notice (and praise) your child's strengths.

6. *Not letting the child take some responsibility for the problem.* Regardless of how much work you're doing to help your child, the problem is the child's to solve, not yours. Motivating children to deal with their problems is difficult and often frustrating. If your child consistently refuses to cooperate, sometimes it's best to let nature take its course. Life experience can be a great teacher.

> Stacey was a little girl whose parents described an endless litany of anxieties and anxiety-related behaviors. She was sensitive to fabrics, so she wore unusual clothes. She was a picky eater. She was up half the night fearing that a burglar would break into the house. The list went on and on, and her family felt overwhelmed. They were told to pick just one fear to work on, preferably the one that interfered most with Stacey's day-to-day activities. The others would have to be tackled later. Stacey and her parents picked the fear of burglars.
>
> Surprisingly, while Stacey was working on the burglar fear, her sensitivity to fabrics resolved as well. Her parents wondered how this could happen. Stacey provided the answer: "It's not cool to dress like I did before." The fear of ridicule by other children had acted as a powerful incentive for Stacey to overcome her sensitivity to fabrics.

When a Technique Stops Working

Sometimes, techniques that work initially appear to stop working after awhile. This does not mean you're back to square one. Remember the natural course of anxiety: It tends to come and go, depending on the balance between (a) your child's coping skills and supports and (b) your child's vulnerability and stressors (see Figure 1). Thus, most treatments for anxiety go two steps forward, one step back as the anxiety remits or exacerbates. When using desensitization, you may encounter a setback when your child hasn't faced the feared situation for awhile or faces it unexpectedly. For example, a child who fears school will tend to do well on Fridays, after four days of exposure, and poorly on Mondays, after two days without exposure. Similarly, a child who has gradually overcome the fear of a friend's dog but sees a strange dog unexpectedly may once again appear fearful. It can take a good deal of patience to persevere despite these ups and downs.

Another common reason for techniques to "not work anymore" is that the child is facing higher expectations. For example, a child who is anxious about school but learns to cope may have a setback when starting high school. This doesn't mean that the child's anxiety has become worse. It simply takes more skills to cope with high school than grade school.

Anticipating the Future

It may be helpful to think for a moment about some stresses or challenges your child is likely to face in the future and how you could help the child adapt to these. Reviewing previously learned coping skills and adding some new ones if necessary are recommended. As before, the child must face what is feared, quickly return to age-appropriate activities, and practice the necessary coping skills until the new challenge has been mastered. If professional help is needed, try to deal with the same professionals who were previously helpful, to ensure continuity in your child's care.

Also, in order to develop into healthy adults, children do not have to face every single thing they fear. Remember the goal of anxiety reduction: to improve the child's ability to function in daily life and allow the child to participate in all age-appropriate activities. Some anxieties are about rare events or situations that have very little effect on daily functioning. A fear of riding roller coasters, for example, interferes with your child's life much less than a fear of going to school. It may not be worth the time and effort involved to desensitize your child to roller coasters. Similarly, children who fear gruesome horror movies often choose to simply avoid this type of movie, with no negative effect on their lives.

Finally, don't underestimate the value of your own increasing confidence as a parent. Some parents have difficulty sticking to the kind of organized, systematic approach described in this book. Because they develop a better under-standing of their child's anxiety, however, they find it easier not to "lose it" when faced with their child's difficult, anxiety-related behaviors. The fact that they are less anxious about the child's problems and more understanding of the child allows the whole family to relax. Because anxious children can be extremely sensitive to conflict around them, a calmer family can go a long way toward reducing these children's anxiety.

APPENDIX

QUESTIONS AND ANSWERS

How can I get my child to tell me what caused the anxiety?

You can't. Many anxious children do not know why they are anxious, and those who do often are embarrassed about it. Spending a great deal of time questioning your child about the problem usually achieves little. In fact, you may make matters worse by focusing too much on the child's weaknesses instead of focusing on the strengths. Instead, label the child's feeling as anxiety, and indicate that this is a perfectly valid feeling: Everyone is anxious sometimes. Then, explore with the child ways of coping with anxiety, perhaps using an example of how you yourself have coped with anxiety. If your child can think of at least one coping strategy that may help, this discovery will reduce anxiety far more than finding a cause.

Could my child's anxiety have been caused by abuse?

Abused children are almost always anxious, but not all anxious children have been abused. If you have evidence that your child has been abused, stop reading this book and notify the appropriate authorities. If you don't have such evidence, however, remember that your child may be vulnerable to anxiety for other reasons. Even minor stressors may provoke anxiety-related behaviors in a child who has always been sensitive. If your child has shown no previous signs of sensitivity, a more significant stressor is required to cause anxiety but it may not necessarily be abuse.

If you are not sure what is making your child anxious, begin by finding out if your child is being bullied or threatened by peers, if there have been problems at school, or if anything in your family is happening to upset the child. Indicate a willingness to listen to your child and to believe what the child says. Whatever the problem is, you are more likely to find the truth through sensitive listening than interrogation.

What if my child's anxiety is caused by deep psychological conflicts? Shouldn't one find the underlying cause of the anxiety rather than just treating the symptoms?

It is difficult to tell whether a child has deep psychological conflicts. Psychoanalytic theories about such conflicts were used for many years in the treatment of anxiety disorders. Studies of these treatments, however, showed that analyzing conflicts without also exposing the anxious people to what they feared had little effect on anxiety. Also, getting these people to face their fears became more difficult the longer a feared situation had been avoided.

Thus, having your child seen in psychotherapy or play therapy to explore psychological conflicts *without* facing what is feared can be detrimental. On the other hand, many anxious children have been successfully treated with the techniques in this book even though nobody ever found an underlying cause. If you feel your child may need psychotherapy, get an opinion from a competent therapist, but do not neglect your child's need to also face what is feared.

How can I give my anxious child self-esteem?

Self-esteem cannot be given to children by their parents, by a therapist, or by anyone else. Self-esteem is built up gradually, based on a child's accumulated experiences over time. Children whose ideas and efforts are consistently valued gradually think of themselves as valuable; children whose ideas and efforts are ridiculed do not. Children who repeatedly master difficult challenges gradually think of themselves as competent; children who are protected from challenges do not. Everything in this book is designed to slowly build self-esteem. Your empathy and encouragement, combined with the child's experience of successfully facing feared situations, will strengthen your child's self-esteem more than any professional intervention.

My child sometimes hyperventilates but then starts to kick and scream when I try to be reassuring. Is this a panic attack?

Probably not. Anxiety can certainly produce hyperventilation, but so can anger. Hyperventilation resulting from anxiety generally involves movements of the shoulders and upper torso. If lower-body movements such as kicking and stomping are also present, the child is probably angry. What you describe, therefore, is more likely to be a tantrum than a panic attack, especially if the child is preadolescent (when true panic attacks are rare). Tantrums resolve when attention is withdrawn from a child. In this situation, stop talking and give the child a few minutes to cool off.

Anxious children can have tantrums that are unrelated to anxiety (as many other children do) or tantrums that result from an overzealous attempt to make them do something they fear. Once children reach school age, they are usually too big for you to make them do anything. Instead, use appropriate pleasant or unpleasant consequences for the child's actions to modify behavior.

What is biofeedback?

Biofeedback is a method of training the body to relax by using information on various physical measures. It has been found that people who are repeatedly provided with information on their heart rate, blood pressure, and skin temperature can learn to control these measures. As they become adept at lowering their heart rate, lowering their blood pressure, and increasing their skin temperature, they become more relaxed. Most biofeedback requires sophisticated equipment, but a mood ring (available at many dollar stores) is a simple biofeedback device for skin temperature. The ring is black when cold, but by doing relaxation while wearing the ring, the child can warm it and make it change color.

With the right treatment, will my child's anxiety be cured?

A cure that eliminates all vulnerability to anxiety is not possible, but anxious children can develop enough coping skills to adapt to a broad range of life experiences. They may have to face new experiences more slowly than other children, but they can still adapt to those experiences. Early on, you may find that your child has a waxing and waning course: coping well for a time and then experiencing anxiety again when facing a new challenge. The goal of treating anxious children is to improve their ability to cope, which decreases their distress and reduces the number of anxious episodes in the long run. Eventually, a new challenge upsets the child briefly (perhaps for a day or two) but does not result in a major setback. In addition, remember that a life completely free from anxiety is unrealistic for anyone. Most people experience some stress, and it isn't necessarily a bad thing. Studies have shown that people perform at their best when mildly stressed.

GLOSSARY

Adrenaline   The body's major stress hormone. It produces the rapid heartbeat, rapid breathing, sweating, and other physical symptoms of fear or anxiety.

Advocating for your child   Educating other people about how to best help your child and making sure they work together to do so. Ongoing collaboration with your child's school (if this is an area of difficulty) is a common example.

Anticipatory anxiety   Worries or feelings of dread about dangerous events that could possibly (but won't necessarily) happen in the future.

Anxiety   A fearful physical, mental, and emotional reaction in the absence of real danger. When it results in the avoidance of a situation that is not dangerous, it is called a *phobia*.

Attachment   The early bond that forms between parents and infants, as parents respond to their infants' distress. Sensitive and reliable responses are thought to result in the most secure attachment relationships.

Behavioral inhibition   That aspect of sensitive children's early temperament thought to make them vulnerable to later anxiety problems. Inhibited children are unusually cautious in approaching new situations and have difficulty adjusting to change.

CBT   Cognitive behavioral therapy, a form of psychotherapy for anxious children that changes anxious feelings by modifying the child's anxious behaviors and anxiety-related thoughts. There is more research evidence for CBT for childhood anxiety than any other form of psychotherapy.

Cognitive distortions   Thought patterns that overemphasize the negative or frightening aspects of situations. Everyone uses them occasionally, but anxious and depressed people use them very frequently.

Coping self-talk   A technique that anxious children and adults can use to put their fears in perspective. It consists of identifying the cognitive distortions that are exaggerating one's fear in a given situation and finding other, more rational ways of looking at the same situation.

Desensitization   A technique for helping children overcome their anxiety about a given situation by repeatedly exposing them to that situation until it is no longer frightening. If done gradually, it is termed *systematic desensitization.* If done suddenly, it is termed *flooding.*

Fight-or-flight response   The body's automatic physical response when sensing danger. It is designed to help a person fight or flee from a dangerous situation and is governed by the sympathetic nervous system.

Incentives and disincentives   Responses to a child's behavior that (respectively) encourage or discourage the repetition of that particular behavior. Anything that increases a particular behavior, even if unpleasant, is considered an incentive.

Level of functioning   A child's ability to engage in age-appropriate activities at home, at school, and with peers. A reduced level of functioning is often found in children who are becoming disabled by their anxieties.

Relaxation response   The body's automatic physical response when sensing no danger. It is designed to reduce a person's level of stress when in safe situations and is governed by the parasympathetic nervous system. Abdominal breathing and other relaxation exercises serve to turn on this response.

SSRI Selective serotonin reuptake inhibitor, a form of antidepressant medication that has been found effective in treating childhood anxiety. SSRI medications are the most commonly used drugs for childhood anxiety.

Transitional objects   Items that symbolize a reassuring parent in a child's mind and can therefore be used by the child for comfort when the parents are not available.

RESOURCES FOR HELPING YOUR ANXIOUS CHILD

Books

Apgras, Stewart, M.D. *Panic: Facing Fears, Phobias, and Anxiety.* New York: W. H. Freeman, 1985. Clinical information on anxiety disorders (adult).

Belknap, Martha, and Ray Kemble. *Taming Your Dragons: A Collection of Creative Relaxation Activities for Home and School.*

New York: Whole Person Assoc., 1994. A variety of relaxation activities for school-aged children.

Berry, Joy. *About Dependence and Separation*. Chicago: Children's Press, 1990. Picture book on separation anxiety (school-age children).

Brett, Doris. *Annie Stories*. New York: Workman Publishing, 1986. Stories parents can read to their anxious children (preschool to early school-age children).

Burns, David, M.D. *Feeling Good*. New York: Penguin Books USA Inc., 1980. Cognitive strategies for anxiety and depression (adult).

Chorpita, Bruce F. *Modular Cognitive Behavioral Therapy for Childhood Anxiety Disorders*. London: Guilford, 2006. Adaptations of cognitive behavioral therapy for children with complex anxiety problems.

Foa, Edna B. *If Your Adolescent Has an Anxiety Disorder: An Essential Resource for Parents*. London: Oxford University Press, 2006. Advice for parents of anxious teens, specific to each anxiety disorder.

Foa, Edna B., and Reid Wilson. *Stop Obsessing! How to Overcome Your Obsessions and Compulsions*. New York: Bantam Books, 2001. Self-help for OCD in adolescents and adults.

Golomb, Ruth Goldfinger, and Sherrie Mansfield Vavrichek. *The Hair Pulling Habit and You: How to Solve the Trichotillomania Puzzle*. London: Writer's Cooperative of Great Britain, 1995. Self-help for children with trichotillomania and their parents.

Greene, Ross W. *The Explosive Child (Revised Edition)*. New York: Harper Paperbacks, 2005. An approach to parenting temperamentally rigid children who often have angry "meltdowns."

Greist, J. H., J. W. Jefferson, and I. M. Marks. *Anxiety and Its Treatment*. Washington, D.C.: American Psychiatric Press, 1986. Clinical information on anxiety disorders (adult).

Kabat-Zinn, Jon. *Mindfulness Meditation Practice CD's*. Available at *www.stressreductiontapes.com*, 2002. Teaches adolescents and adults how to relax the mind by focusing on one's breathing.

Lewis, David, M.D. *Helping Your Anxious Child*. London: Reed Consumer Books, 1988. Addresses mainly school-related childhood anxieties, using a behavioral approach (adult).

Manassis, Katharina, and Anne-Marie Levac. *Helping Your Teenager Beat Depression: A Problem-Solving Approach for Families.* Bethesda, MD: Woodbine House, 2004. A guide to help parents of depressed teens support their recovery.

March, John S., and Christine M. Benton. *Talking Back to OCD.* London: Guilford, 2006. Self-help for children and adolescents with OCD, including guidance for parents.

McHolm, Angela E., Charles E. Cunningham, Melanie K. Vanier, and Ronald Rapee. *Helping Your Child with Selective Mutism.* New York: New Harbinger, 2005. Guide to help parents support their selectively mute children's recovery.

Morgan, Roger, Ph.D. *Behavioral Treatments with Children.* London: William Heinemann Medical Books, 1984. Case examples of how children with various emotional problems can be helped through behavior modification (adult).

Murdock, Maureen. *Spinning Inward.* Boston: Shambhala Publications, 1987. Relaxing, imagery-based meditations for children.

Phelan, Thomas W., Ph.D. *1-2-3 Magic.* Book or videotape available by mail. Write to Thomas W. Phelan, Ph.D., Child Management Inc., 800 Roosevelt Road, Glen Ellyn, IL 60137. Offers a more detailed description of time-outs and other strategies for managing defiant behavior (adult).

Rapoport, Judith L., M.D. *The Boy Who Couldn't Stop Washing.* New York: Dutton, 1989. Case examples and information about Obsessive-Compulsive Disorder (adult).

Timmons, Bonnie, *Anxiety.* New York: Fawcett Columbine, 1991. Cartoons about anxiety (all ages).

Turecki, Stanley, M.D., and Sarah Wernick, Ph.D. *The Emotional Problems of Normal Children.* New York: Bantam Books, 1994. Advice on managing normal children with difficult temperaments. Not specific to anxiety but presents a number of good principles of child management (adult).

Organizations: United States

American Academy of Child and Adolescent Psychiatry
AACAP Public Information, P.O. Box 96106,
Washington, D.C. 20090-6106. Tel.: (800) 333-7636
(provides a bulletin, *Facts for Families:* ask for #47, "Anxious Child")

Anxiety Disorders Association of America
6000 Executive Boulevard, Suite 513
Rockville, MD, 20852. Tel.: (301) 231-9350
(newsletter; state listings of treatment providers who specialize in
   anxiety disorders)

National Institute of Mental Health
Public Inquiries, Room 7C-02, 5600 Fishers Lane,
Rockville, MD 20857. Tel.: (301) 443-4513
(resource list of books, videos, articles on panic disorder and related
   anxieties)

National Mental Health Association
(800) 969-6642
(clearinghouse; referral data base)

Organizations: Canada

Canadian Mental Health Association
2160 Yonge Street, Toronto. Tel.: (416) 484-7750
(General information on anxiety; also, temperature biofeedback cards
   available)

Dorothy C. Madgett Relaxation Clinic
123 Edward Street, Toronto. Tel.: (416) 340-7070
(courses in relaxation, covered by the Ontario Health Insurance Plan
   (OHIP) with doctor's prescription)

Eli Bay's Relaxation Response Institute
858 Eglinton Avenue West, Toronto. Tel.: (416) 789-7261
(courses in relaxation; relaxation tapes)

INDEX

Abdominal breathing, 66–67
Absences from school, 115–117
Abuse, 108, 174
Addiction, 92
Adolescents
  anxiety in, 107–110
  panic attacks in, 117–119
Age-appropriate expectations, 157
Alcohol abuse, 108
Amotivational syndrome, 93
Anticipation, 8, 50, 172–173
Antidepressants, 85, 88–90, 93, 118–119
Anxiety
  about current events, 142–144
  case studies of, 3–4
  definition of, 8, 17, 41
  development of, 10–14
  externalizing of, 57
  facts about, 57–58
  gender predilection of, 12
  labeling of, 56–57
  long-term consequences of, 97
  misconceptions about, 160
  natural course of, 171–172
  over life span, 14
  overwhelming, 72
  prevalence of, 10
  range of, 3–6
  reduction of, 84
  severity of, 4–6
  talking about, 174
Anxiety-provoking situations, 59

Anxious feelings, 34–35
Arbitrary inference, 51
Attention, 39
Attitude
  differences in, 154–157
  encouraging, 22–23
  range of, 153–154

Baseline, 23–24
Behavior
  changing of, 101
  defiant, 45–47
  fearful. See Fearful behaviors
Behavioral inhibition, 10
Benzodiazepines, 90–92
Biofeedback, 176
Breathing, 63, 66–67
Bribe, 42
Buspirone, 92

Caffeine, 73
Change
  coping with, 78–82
  fallacies of, 52
  in teenagers, 110
Chorpita, Bruce, 59
Clingy child, 111–114
Clomipramine, 89
Cognitive behavioral therapy, 59
Collaboration, 161–162
Communication, 149–150, 155, 158
Community
  collaboration with others, 161–162
  schoolteachers, 162–164
  telling others about your child's problem, 159–161
Competence, 53
Concentration, 70
Confidence
  building of, 21–27

of parent, 173
Consistency
  in family interactions, 149–152
  importance of, 153–158, 170
Coping
  with change, 78–82
  independent, 60–61
  methods of, 94
  modeling of, 54, 63
  sensitivity and, 12–14
  support and, 10–11
Coping self-talk, 53, 55–56, 58–59, 63, 99, 131
Coping skills
  description of, 14
  for teenagers, 109
Coping thoughts, 54

Day-to-day activities, 96
Defiant behavior, 45–47
Depression, 35, 108, 110, 169
Desensitization
  definition of, 21–22
  exposures, 30–31
  gradual, 29–31
  long-term consequences of anxiety prevented through, 97
  medication and, 85
  questions about, 32–35
  for rituals, 132
  systematic, 28–31
  techniques for, 28–31
  transitional object and, 113
  for trichotillomania, 134
Desirable behaviors, 37
Developmental delays, 12
Dichotomous thinking, 51–52

182

Diet, 73–75
Dissatisfaction with professionals, 166–167
Distraction, 50, 99–100

Early relationships, 10–12
Emotional reasoning, 52
Empathy, 155
Encouragement, 22–23, 28, 100, 109
Endorphins, 75
Exercise, 75
Expectations, 157, 171–172
Explosive outbursts, 47
Exposures, desensitization, 30-31

Fairness, 52
Fallacies, 52
Family arguments, 40
Family interactions
    communication, 149–150
    consistency in, 149–152
    examples of, 147–149
    flexibility in, 149, 151
    incentive systems and, 39–40
Family therapy, 98
Fear(s)
    definition of, 17
    description of, 15–16
    phobias and, 16–17
    setbacks in handling, 34
    unrealistic, 17
FEAR mnemonic, 59, 61
Fearful behaviors
    baseline of, 23–24
    inability to control, 43
    physical symptoms with, 43
    progress in changing, 25–27
Fight-of-flight reaction, 7–8, 14, 21, 66, 118
Flooding, 28–29, 115
Fluoxetine, 89
Fluvoxamine, 89
Future, anticipation of, 172–173

Generalized anxiety disorder, 49
Gradual desensitization, 29–31
Group therapy, 98

Helplessness, 138
Hospitalizations, 77
Hyperventilation, 67, 175

Incentives/incentive systems
    benefits of, 39–40
    family interaction effects on, 39
    praise, 36, 44
    principles of, 37–39
    questions about, 41–44
    rewards, 37–39, 41–42
    for selective mutism, 124
    for sleeping alone, 114
    for trichotillomania, 135
Independent coping, 60–61
Introducing new situations, 79

"Just in case" plan, 79

Kabat-Zinn, Jon, 70
Kendall, Philip, 59, 61

Loss of privileges, 46, 116
Lying, 140–141

Magnification, 51
Medications
    addiction concerns, 92
    antidepressants, 85, 88–90, 93, 118–119
    benefits of, 84–85
    benzodiazepines, 90–92
    course of treatment, 92–93
    growth concerns, 93
    limitations of, 100
    side effects of, 86
    when to consider, 83–87
Meditation, 71
Mind focusing, 70–71
Minimization, 51

Modeling of thoughts, 54, 63
Modular, 59

Negative emotions, 72, 170

Obsessions, 129–133
Obsessive-compulsive disorder, 88, 129–133
Overgeneralization, 51
Overprotection, 158

Pain, 68–69
Panic, 23
Panic attacks, 35, 85, 117–119, 175–176
Panic disorder, 118
Parasympathetic nervous system, 66
Parental confidence, 173
Parental praise, 36, 44
Perfectionism, 42, 137–138
Personalization, 52
Phelan, Thomas, 46
Phobia
    definition of, 17
    fears and, 16–17
    school, 115
    sharing information with child, 32
    triggering events, 18
Physical disorders, 76–77
Positive reinforcement, 109
Post-traumatic stress disorder, 143–144
Praise, 36, 44, 122
Predictability, 78–80
Procrastination, 138–140
Professionals, 165–169
Progress
    charting of, 38
    description of, 25–27
    evaluation of, 44
Progressive muscle relaxation, 67
Psychological conflicts, 175
Psychotherapy, 98, 175

Reality testing, 56, 62
Reality-based fear, 95
Reinforcements, 44, 100
Relationships, early, 10–12
Relaxation
  description of, 7, 58
  limitations of, 99
  techniques of, 65–69
  in young child, 106
Response prevention, 132
Rewards, 37–39, 41–43
Ritalin, 93
Rituals, 129–133
Role-play, 122, 126
Routines, 78

School phobia, 115
School refusal, 115–117
Schoolteachers, 162–164
Selective abstraction, 51
Selective mutism, 123–124
Selective serotonin
  reuptake inhibitors, 89,
  125
Self-esteem, 39, 108, 175
Self-identity, 107
Self-responsibility, 171
Self-talk, coping, 53,
  55–56, 58–59, 63, 99,
  131
Senses, 81
Sensitivity
  coping and, 12–14
  origins of, 7–9
Separation anxiety
  disorder, 111
Serotonin, 85
Setbacks, 34, 117, 171–172
"Shoulds" fallacies, 52
Shyness, 120–125

Silence, 120–125
Single-parent households,
  157
Sleep, 75–76
Sleeping alone, 113–114
Social skills, 121–122
Stress reduction
  description of, 13
  relaxation techniques
  for, 65–69
Stressful events, 63–64
Suicide, 35, 89
Support
  amount of, 33
  coping and, 10–11
  for young child, 105
Sympathetic nervous
  system, 7–8, 66, 73
Systematic desensitization,
  28–31

Talking, 47
Tantrums, 40, 175–176
Teachers. See
  Schoolteachers
Teasing, 127–128
Teenagers, 107–110
Temper tantrums, 40,
  175–176
Thinking
  coping thoughts, 54
  worried, 49–53
Tics, 136
Time-outs, 46–47
Tourette's syndrome,
  136
Traits, 5
Transitional object, 113
Treatments
  goals of, 166, 172, 176

medications. See
  Medications
  obstacles to success,
  170–173
  relaxation. See
  Relaxation
  setbacks in, 171–172
Trichotillomania, 134–136
Tricyclic antidepressants,
  89

Unassertiveness, 126–128
Undesirable behaviors, 37
Unexpected situations,
  82
Unrealistic expectations,
  171
Unrealistic fear, 17, 96

Visualization, 71
Vulnerability, 153–154

"What if?" questions, 48,
  55
Withdrawal of rewards,
  46
Worrying
  about rewards, 42–43
  cognitive distortions,
  51–52
  coping techniques,
  55–59
  examples of, 48–49
  thinking associated with,
  49–53
  in young child, 62–63

Young child
  anxiety in, 105–106
  worrying in, 62–63